CHIVALRY

THE QUEST
FOR A PERSONAL
CODE OF HONOR
IN AN UNJUST
WORLD

ZACH
HUNTER

TYNDALE™
MOMENTUM

AN IMPRINT OF TYNDALE HOUSE PUBLISHERS, INC.

Visit Tyndale online at www.tyndale.com.

Visit Tyndale Momentum online at www.tyndalemomentum.com.

TYNDALE is a registered trademark of Tyndale House Publishers, Inc. *Tyndale Momentum* and the Tyndale Momentum logo are trademarks of Tyndale House Publishers, Inc. Tyndale Momentum is an imprint of Tyndale House Publishers, Inc.

Chivalry: The Quest for a Personal Code of Honor in an Unjust World

Copyright © 2013 by Zach Hunter. All rights reserved.

Cover and interior photograph of forest copyright © Chase Jarvis/Getty. All rights reserved.

Interior photograph of the author speaking copyright © Marc Gilgen/marcgilgen.com. All rights reserved.

All other interior photographs are copyright © Zach Hunter. All rights reserved.

Author photograph by Alex Parva, copyright © 2012. All rights reserved.

Designed by Dean H. Renninger

Edited by Jeremy V. Jones

Unless otherwise indicated, all Scripture quotations are taken from the *Holy Bible,* New Living Translation, copyright © 1996, 2004, 2007 by Tyndale House Foundation. Used by permission of Tyndale House Publishers, Inc., Carol Stream, Illinois 60188. All rights reserved.

Scripture quotations marked NIV are taken from the Holy Bible, *New International Version,*® *NIV.*® Copyright © 1973, 1978, 1984, 2011 by Biblica, Inc.™ (Some quotations may be from the previous NIV edition, copyright © 1984.) Used by permission of Zondervan. All rights reserved worldwide. www.zondervan.com.

Scripture quotations marked *The Message* are taken from *The Message* by Eugene H. Peterson, copyright © 1993, 1994, 1995, 1996, 2000, 2001, 2002. Used by permission of NavPress Publishing Group. All rights reserved.

Scripture quotations marked ASV are taken from *The Holy Bible*, American Standard Version.

Scripture quotations marked ESV are taken from *The Holy Bible*, English Standard Version® (ESV®), copyright © 2001 by Crossway, a publishing ministry of Good News Publishers. Used by permission. All rights reserved.

Scripture quotations marked NASB are from the New American Standard Bible,® copyright © 1960, 1962, 1963, 1968, 1971, 1972, 1973, 1975, 1977, 1995 by The Lockman Foundation. Used by permission.

Some names and other identifying details of people mentioned in this book have been changed to safeguard the privacy of the individuals involved.

Library of Congress Cataloging-in-Publication Data

Hunter, Zach.
    Chivalry : the quest for a personal code of honor in an unjust world / by Zach Hunter.
        pages cm
    Includes bibliographical references.
    ISBN 978-1-4143-7635-6 (pbk.)
    1. Christian life.   2. Conduct of life.   I. Title.
    BV4501.3.H867 2013
    241.5—dc23   2013004470

Printed in the United States of America

19   18   17   16   15   14   13
7   6   5   4   3   2   1

For love.

CONTENTS

AN EPIC QUEST

"We live in a wonderful world that is full of beauty, charm, and adventure. There is no end to the adventures that we can have if only we seek them with our eyes open."

JAWAHARLAL NEHRU
FIRST PRIME MINISTER OF INDIA

So, maybe you picked up this book, and despite the subtitle, thought it would be a how-to book teaching guys how to treat girls.

Or maybe you thought it would be a book about sexual abstinence or manliness.

We're actually going to go on a much more difficult journey together—a quest to be chivalrous people. Not just guys. Not just girls. But chivalrous, civil *people*. People who live by a code of honor.

My generation is tired of talk—I believe we will be known as a generation of action. We want to see real answers and be a part of the solution to some of the biggest problems facing the globe. I have spent much of the past eight years talking about social justice and the call to demonstrate sacrificial Love to the world by relieving the suffering of the poor and oppressed—specifically, helping in the fight to end modern-day slavery.

As I've pursued this goal, I've noticed a double standard in many people's lives, including my own. And I've become concerned. Concerned that . . .

while great progress is being made in the fight against poverty;

while more and more people are getting involved in
    helping their fellow humans who are hungry, sick,
    oppressed, or uneducated;
while social justice is once again becoming a common
    outworking of the Christian faith . . .

I'm seeing less civil and kind behavior in many people's personal lives.

Basically, I think we're a generation in conflict. Conflicted in ourselves. We often think we have crystal-clear vision about the problems "out there," but I'm concerned that we are forgetting to look "in here"—inside our hearts and minds where real character is revealed. Could it be that we're a generation of activists who are spiritual anorexics? Could it be that we're spending a lot of time being busy with our world-changing projects and forgetting about the spiritual transformation that may take even more time, more dedication, and more discipline? And that in the process, our personal lives don't reflect the world-changer, compassion-driven labels our social media pages may declare?

I've noticed that there is a meanness and lack of respect being demonstrated in close personal relationships by those of us who are concentrating on living out our faith farther from home, among those we don't know well. And all we have to do is look at the Halls of Power to see daily demonstrations of uncivilized arguing and name-calling.

If "justice is what love looks like in public,"[1] as Princeton professor Dr. Cornel West puts it, then I wonder if chivalry and civility are what justice looks like in private. Private justice as opposed to social justice.

This brand of justice goes beyond caring about what is trendy, to caring about who we are as people and how we treat others.

So why should we care about this idea of chivalry?

While we are caring for the poor, loving our neighbors, and fighting to right wrongs committed against each other, we want our lives up close to be consistent with that life marked by compassion and chivalry.

Knights in shining armor are scarce these days. But heroes are all around us—and maybe even inside us.

We're going to turn this old notion of chivalry upside down and make it about men *and* women. We're going to tear down old ideas about only men having the responsibility to be chivalrous and instead imagine a society that is civil—both male and female.

Make no mistake, chivalry is not about learning how to be nice. Too many Christians are taught to focus on being pleasant and polite rather than being chivalrous. Young women are often under pressure to "act ladylike," while young men are ordered to "be gentlemen." At times, the pursuit of being more like Jesus can even take a backseat to being proper and nice. That's a problem, since being "nice" is just external behavior. True kindness is of the Spirit, it's internal, and it's lasting. It's not just Southern politeness (bless your heart!), but enduring and transcendent love.

That means actually being civil to people because you *want* to be, not because they can do something for you or because you are supposed to be.

When I mention civility, I'm not talking about rules like men opening doors for women or the how-to's of courting or dating or "keeping yourself pure." I don't know about you, but I'm tired of hearing lists of what I should and shouldn't do. What I should and shouldn't eat or drink. What I should and shouldn't watch, touch, or say. This book isn't about those rules.

Instead, this book is built around a code I've crafted from ten of the principles the knights lived by. If lived out today, this code would change us so dramatically that those around us would have to take notice. *Chivalry* is about how we should *be*—the transformation that takes place internally as we open up every area of our lives to be conformed to something that is not of this world: the image of an amazing, terrifying, all-consuming, and all-loving God who gives without limit and sacrifices without end. This is where we will lose ourselves and find a code that is higher and longer lasting than any pledge we may make.

I hope you'll set off on this journey with me. It won't be easy. I have not even come close to living out all of these principles. But I am dedicating my life to the process. And something I've discovered is that the closer we get to people and the more willing we are to be transformed, the more we uncover about becoming more chivalrous and civil.

Let the quest begin.

Zach Hunter
JANUARY 2013

I WILL NOT GO ON THIS JOURNEY ALONE.

"DEEP ROOTS ARE NOT REACHED BY THE FROST."

J. R. R. TOLKIEN

ROOTED

CARLOS HAS LOVED TREES since the time he tried to grow one when he was in grade school. He had seen the tiny tree breaking through the cracks in the asphalt in front of his school bus stop. That afternoon he took the little tree home and planted it in the sandy vacant lot next to his apartment building. He had visions of it growing into a big tree like the ones he had seen in a textbook—trees with faucets stuck into the bark by people who would draw out syrup for pancakes. Carlos's sapling died within days.

Even so, trees fascinated him. He grew up in Los Angeles, however, and never even visited a forest until he was seventeen. By then he had saved up enough money flipping burgers to buy his uncle's old Dodge Dart. He bought a map at the corner market and charted his course to the Angeles National Forest by tracing the lines with a black ballpoint pen. The width of his thumbnail, according to the key on the map, was roughly five miles. Using this as a gauge, he was able to determine that the forest was about twenty miles away.

He couldn't believe the new world he saw as he drove the Angeles Crest Highway. Green grasses and brilliantly colored wildflowers. Mountains taller than any buildings, stabbing into the sky, silhouetted, looking almost like dark rips in the light-blue sky. Animals walking around like they owned the place.

And trees! Trees whispering to one another. Carlos wished he could understand them. That was when he fell in love with trees. If he had been infatuated before, now he was in love. The honeymoon never ended.

Several years later Carlos met a girl named Graciela. She was one of the few people who didn't find it strange that Carlos lit up inside when he talked about hearing trees talk to each other, about how people are like trees with roots that don't take so long to move. She shared his glow when he dreamed of owning a nice little cottage where their children and grandchildren could play beneath the lovely shade trees.

Carlos married Graciela at Angeles National Forest in the autumn beneath a big tree that was shedding its colorful tissue-paper leaves. It was nestled in an evergreen stand where the giants towered over and protected it.

The couple shared many good years. Carlos worked a steady job at the local fertilizer plant. He and Graciela raised their twins, Aspen and Abeto, in the white cottage that they built.

Now Carlos lived there alone. The twins had their own families. Graciela had passed long ago. He missed her, but the whisper of the trees they had planted together in the yard brought him happy memories. Carlos knew he had learned more about life from Graciela and from trees than he had learned from any book.

One day Aspen brought her family to visit. Her son Ash was nearly the same age Carlos had been when he first stepped into the forest so many years before. Carlos listened as his grandson boasted about the city and his plans to make it big there. He couldn't wait to leave home.

Carlos led Ash outside and pointed to the tree he and Graciela had planted the spring after the boy had been born.

"When a young tree is planted, it is at risk of being whipped about by the wind," Carlos explained, pointing to the sturdy trunk. "If the sapling is tied to a single stake and pulled in one direction, it will grow up leaning hard to that side. It will be uprooted by a storm or grow crooked. That's why it's important to stake a tree from multiple directions. The tension on three different sides helps a tree grow straight and true. Its roots will deepen, its trunk will strengthen, and it will bear much fruit. With the right support, a tree will grow to be a glorious thing."

Carlos looked at his grandson. "Trees and humans are not so different from each other."

I have a friend named Stayko (pronounced *STY-coe*). Almost every time I see him, he's wearing a bow tie and a mile-wide grin. In conversation, he acts like you are the most important person he has ever met.

Once when I was in the car with him, I overheard him conducting a Russian oil deal. That was interesting. He's one of those guys who could be in his home in Washington, DC, one day and the next pop in for a meeting in New York, Chicago, or London. He could live anywhere, but before he was married, Stayko chose to live in an apartment with some other guys. He didn't have to, but he decided to live in community because he felt that this is where boys become men and where humanity takes form.

It was from Stayko that I learned about this concept of being a young sapling staked in many directions. He gave me this advice at the National Prayer Breakfast in Washington, DC, when I was sixteen. Stayko told me about his mentors and about the young men he had invited into his life to walk closely with him. They were all from unique backgrounds, had various political opinions, and were experts in different areas. He explained how much he needed these diverse influences, just like a growing tree needs multiple stakes to grow tall and straight. He warned of trying to go it alone.

If you are very interested in one thing, Stayko told me, it is easy to try to find a single mentor who is very good at that one thing. In fact, it can be tempting to surround yourself with people who also share that same interest. But that is a mistake that many people make—it pulls them away from being well rounded and makes them vulnerable to tough times. With a variety of people providing the stakes in the ground, holding us in tension and securing us from swaying one way or another, we will flourish.

"We stand, many minds, backgrounds, and voices—but one heart. Accepting the charge to lead, to follow, to influence, to build community. We want to do more than succeed. We want to be significant."

AMENA BROWN, "BE THE ONE"

FRIENDS FOR THE JOURNEY

We were all born with relational needs. Science backs this idea. Babies who don't get enough human contact may grow up having to overcome serious emotional issues.

But we like to pretend we're self-sufficient. It's pretty easy to think we're set in life, that we have it all together in many areas, that we really don't need anyone else. I've seen communities of people where nobody encourages anyone else to grow or change for the better. When I've been involved in those communities,

I just felt really stuck—not moving forward, not finding adventure and joy. If you're in that situation now, it may be time for you to branch out, to seek companionship with a group of people who will lift you up when you are down.

On the other hand, you may be like me in another way. For much of my life, I've had a hard time making friends. It's probably because I'm an introvert. I like being around people—but I don't get my energy from that. Sometimes I feel like my thought processes are different from those of most people, and that others just don't get me. In fact, from talking with a coach and counselor who has helped me a lot, I've learned that I may have always dealt with a kind of social anxiety or social awkwardness. And it has actually been reassuring, because it helps me make sense of my occasional challenges in building relationships. People act surprised when I say that I'm an introvert, since I seem outgoing and my work as a speaker requires that I be. Connecting with people is easier now than it used to be, but it can still be a struggle.

If you can relate to feeling awkward or like you don't fit in, it's really important that you practice being yourself with people. That may sound hard and scary, and it can be. You will mess up and probably make a fool of yourself. At least, I have. But I can tell you that finding meaningful community is *worth it*. Now I have a great group of friends who bring valuable perspective to my life. From the outside looking in, they can help me see things that are in my blind spots. Friends like that can help you avoid heartaches they've already been through. And after you've been friends with them long enough, they can interpret life's challenges for you in a way you can understand, because they *know you*. They know what you've been through, they know what your weaknesses are, and they care about you.

I'm grateful for these close friends God has given me. Our relationships have been carved out of tough times, unusual circumstances, and unlikely places. Some of them I call "brother" or "sister," because they really do feel like family. These are people who know me well enough to tell me the truth about myself; to provide support and encouragement when they know I need it. I value the time I get to spend with them. By now, I know that if my phone rings and I'm hoping their names don't show up on my caller ID, I'm probably going through something that I really need them for.

MENTORS FOR THE JOURNEY

In addition to having a group of authentic friends, it is important to seek wise mentors—people to whom we can be accountable, people who can serve as guides, people who've been where we're going and have made it out alive. Having someone who's older than you who can serve as a mentor is beneficial in a variety of ways. Mentors can still be your friends, but the relationship has a different dynamic. They should be willing to tell you the truth without fear of losing your friendship, because they care about you and your personal growth. They can give perspective and sage advice that comes from their own mistakes and experiences.

I have a group of mentors I call my "personal advisory board." I recommend having one of your own, even if you aren't working in the business world. No matter what your goals are, mentors can help you stay on track.

My goal is to meet with my advisory board once a quarter. Trust me, this isn't easy. I have to intentionally schedule this time, or it won't happen. These guys are all busy people with full calendars, and it takes some effort to coordinate everyone's schedules. But these meetings are so important, it's worth the trouble.

Because my mentors are there for accountability, I don't try to limit their influence. They can ask me anything they want. They're in my life for my own protection and to provide advice.

The key to having helpful mentoring relationships is to think about it like the story of the stakes and the tree. I purposefully chose a diverse group so I would get balanced advice from multiple angles. All of my mentors are from different walks of life and have unique areas of expertise. Leighton is a graphic designer; Charles is a businessman; Randy is a pastor; and Mark is a lot of things (illusionist, executive director, author, and home chef). Mentors from various backgrounds can speak to you and guide you on specific issues, helping you develop and grow. Like the artist mentor, the business mentor, the spiritual mentor—together, their knowledge rounds out your areas of interest.

My dad has always been one of my key mentors. He's the chairman of my advisory board, and he's always available when I need him. I rely heavily on his advice and guidance in my life.

WHEN THE NEED IS GREATEST

On your quest for chivalry, there will be struggles. When you're physically weak, tired, or not feeling well; when you've suffered a loss or setback; when you're going through something difficult or feeling like a failure, your tendency might be to hide or run from your friends and mentors. Or when you've had a major success, you may feel like you don't need them. But you do. In these situations, you need to let in the people who care about you. Don't try to do it on your own—even when you feel strong. This is why I've made a commitment not to travel alone when I go to speak at different events. I always bring someone with me because these events can bring emotional highs and lows.

Chivalrous people aren't foolishly confident, believing they don't need anyone else on this journey. They realize they are human, weak, and vulnerable. They know that strength comes from conditioning and from wise counsel. They want to grow in their faith and be transformed, and they know that this process often requires the messiness of relationships. You have to allow others to get close to you—close enough that they can see your flaws.

A chivalrous person makes a commitment not to go on this quest alone.

I WILL
NEVER
ATTACK
FROM
BEHIND.

"A DISHONEST MAN SPREADS STRIFE, AND A WHISPERER SEPARATES CLOSE FRIENDS."

PROVERBS 16:28, ESV

THE UNDOING

CATARINA SAT IN HER KITCHEN, reading the same line over and over again. Yet the words meant nothing. Her mind had been taken captive by something else.

It's not as though I am the first person ever to do this, she reasoned within herself. *Or that I taught myself to do it. I must have learned it somewhere. It's not really my fault—everyone has done this.* But she couldn't avoid the heaviness in her heart. The restlessness that made sleep elusive. The guilt that made it difficult to face her reflection in the window. Yes, she knew that what she had done was wrong. Even if she hadn't intended for it to go this far. She hadn't seen the harm in her actions until it was too late.

Catarina's peaceful life was unraveling. Her best friends wouldn't talk to her. She knew she had to make it right. She had to go to the one place where deeds could meet freedom, where forgiveness could find a home in her heart.

Gathering her cloak about her, she slipped out the front door. The wind pulled her to the cobblestone streets worn with footsteps and time and wooden carriage wheels. She ducked her head to avoid the assault of the wind—or perhaps the gaze of the too-familiar faces.

She bustled toward the church, barely lifting her feet, her skirt skimming the stones. Wrapping her hand around the cold iron pull, she heaved the wooden door open. As she stepped into the sanctuary, she knew this was where she needed to be.

Determined to rid herself of her stifling burden, she swept herself behind the heavy curtain of the confessional. The fragrance of incense from the morning's mass smelled of guilt and forgiveness blended together. What she carried in and what she hoped to leave with.

"Father, forgive me for I have sinned."

"Child." It was Father Felipe Neri.

She began spilling syllables into the air. "I didn't think it was anything of consequence. I heard things about some friends of mine. Rumors. Some about married people who were seen with others. Instead of going to my friends and asking them, I told people whose business it was not. Now I can't sleep. I can't eat. I can't think about anything else. I only told the truth—or what I thought to be the truth. I didn't intend to wound. But the stories took flight and . . ." Slowing down and taking a breath, she continued, "Indeed, I have hurt many, but that's why I have come to you asking for penance."

A period of silence passed. "My child, I have heard your confession. Here is what you must do. Go to the market and purchase a chicken, the finest you can find. Do not have it cleaned or prepared for a meal. After they have killed it, take it as it is, feathers and all. Journey throughout the town, pluck feathers from the chicken, and drop them on the streets."

"Father, I came for penance, for freedom from my guilt. I would pray. I would apologize. Are you mocking me?"

"Of course you should pray. Of course you should right the wrongs you have committed. But understand, I do not mock. This is your penance. Now go."

Catarina stepped out from the confessional and back into the street. The same wind that had swept her in now swept her away. Still uncertain about the penance, she headed to the market.

The noise of the streets allowed her to focus on her task and not the people. She found the chickens at the back of the market and chose the first one quickly, without really looking. She asked to have it killed but not cleaned. No, she wanted the feathers, thank you. No, not in a sack for stuffing, but left on the chicken. A strange request.

She put the chicken in a basket and wound through the village, plucking the feathers one by one, tossing them into the air. She watched as some blew away in the wind, some were trampled in the mud, some stuck to people's backs, and some flew high and out of sight. In the matter of a few hours, not a feather remained. She had done what was required of her, as absurd as it seemed.

The next morning, fresh and rested, Catarina splashed her face with cold water from the pump. She snatched a hard roll from the bread basket and rushed out the door. She wanted to be free of her guilt. She repeated her journey to the church, wrenching open the heavy door. Once again she walked straight to the confessional, sliding into its privacy on the hard chair.

"Father, I have completed my penance."

"You have done what I asked?"

"Yes."

"Good, child. But you are not yet finished."

"But I did everything you required!" she exclaimed, astonished. "I bought a chicken and had it killed but not cleaned. I scattered the feathers. I saw them float away in the wind or land in the mud. I didn't leave a single feather on the bird. What have I left undone? What is not yet finished?"

Father Felipe paused and let Catarina's questions hang in the air. "You have not finished. You have completed your task, your penance, but there is one more thing you must do. Go and gather every single feather you scattered—do not miss a single one— and then return to me."

"But Father, I have told you I saw the feathers blown far and wide. Some are probably in another village by now. Some are stuck in trees. How can I gather the feathers again? That is impossible."

"Yes, it is. Just as impossible as taking back all the words you have spoken about your friends."

Then Catarina understood. And she knew what she must do.

CLOAK AND DAGGER

Backstabbing. Gossip. Malicious sarcasm. Attacking from behind.

These are all modern manifestations of an ancient problem. A quick text message about someone who's "weird," a biting comment on a Facebook picture, a passing remark meant to wound. These are not the ways of honor and chivalry. We need to learn how to be faithful and loyal to our friends—then try to do the same with our enemies.

An old gunfighter once told me, "Never sit with your back to the door." Actually my dad told me that. But it does refer to a time in the Old American West. In that context, there's something dusty and romantic about it. It sounds like the type of thing Clint Eastwood would mumble from beneath a sweat-stained cowboy hat. In those days, most people were packing heat, and if you cheated at poker or insulted somebody, you ran the risk of ending up on the ground with a bullet in you.

Yet back in the Old West, most people followed one familiar rule: don't shoot anyone in the back. Even bounty hunters, tracking down outlaws for cash (a seemingly less-than-honorable occupation), were supposed to arrest them or at least give them a chance to surrender. Famously, the Confederate outlaw Jesse James was shot in the back of the head by Robert Ford, a member of his own gang. Ford lived in James's house, and reports say that he killed him for the money. Even skilled gunslingers paid the price with their lives when their backs were left unguarded.

Are we still as vulnerable today? I'm not talking about actual physical injury, but about words uttered behind our backs—with or without intent to harm. If we're not around when someone speaks about us, we can't see what's coming. Friends or acquaintances can say just about anything they want about us, and we can't immediately dispute their claims, prove them wrong, or defend ourselves in any way. We're at their mercy, and we don't even know it.

EVERYONE'S A CRITIC

In our culture, it seems that everyone is a critic. We make a hobby out of watching TV shows and criticizing the talents of people much more skilled than we are. We even get to vote on who is the best. We create celebrities and then watch for their failure. We choose to glorify or condemn these people, judging them based on how we feel about them or their fans. This feels so easy, so natural, we might not even realize we're doing it. By choosing to participate in and encourage this type of criticism, we reduce what I have heard called our "mutual humanity."

I have a lot of friends who are successful, people who are well known in the entertainment and music industries. Sometimes I'm asked, "Do you know any celebrities?" or "Who is the most famous person you know?" These kinds of questions bother me because they take a real human being—a living, breathing person with thoughts, feelings, and dreams—and diminish him or her to a piece of gossip. I understand this interest to a point, but I'm often frustrated by the desire people have to know the famous—and to know as much about them as possible.

I still can't believe that tabloids are in business; they are simply purveyors of gossip and rumor. When I glance over the magazine racks at the checkout line, I usually think, *Who cares?* And then I realize: millions do. These trashy magazines are so successful because we love to hear other people's "dirt"—their secrets, their problems, their embarrassing escapades. It's this propensity that leads many to become gossip merchants themselves. People love being the ones who know stuff, especially private information about other people. It allows them to be the center of attention, if only for a moment.

This dehumanization of people in the limelight leaks over into our daily lives, where we can become critical, unkind, and backstabbing.

How does this backstabbing idea relate to the knights' code of chivalry? Back in the day, it was quite literal. As a matter of honor, knights would only violently engage an enemy who was attacking them first. They would never dream of attacking from behind.

The justification of violence in any era is pretty dodgy. But when it came to the code of the knights, these guys had to be prepared to defend themselves. They lived a militant lifestyle. Knights had swords strapped to their sides, much the way lawmen and outlaws carried guns in the Old West. These men were always armed.

To keep themselves from being obsessed with power or being needlessly violent, they set parameters for themselves. They weren't strangers to combat, violence, and even death. Political structures were in shambles, and power had to be maintained and managed lest it be misused—at least, that was the reasoning. But it was in their code *not* to attack needlessly. *Not* to attack from behind. They wouldn't engage someone who was a noncombatant or unarmed.

Sure, it would have been easier for them to identify and attack their enemies while they were sleeping. Bring someone down a couple of notches with guerrilla tactics. A midnight ambush. Assassination. But that wasn't what the knights did. They wouldn't slip someone a blade in a literal cloak-and-dagger manner. They didn't attack unless someone was using violence against them first. Which really isn't attacking—it's called self-defense.

This principle of the knight's lifestyle is extremely applicable today. We don't attack. Period.

That sounds simple enough, right? If necessary, we may choose to engage in a debate. But even then, we don't attack the *person*. Instead, we should use the "weapon" that is available to us—the truth—to defend graciously what is good or beautiful, including other people. Too many times, when we are offended or angry, even on someone else's behalf, we quickly draw our swords and begin hacking away haphazardly with our words. A good discipline to develop is listening to understand others, rather than half-listening in preparation to say the next thing.

Although we may not carry swords like the knights did, we can become armed when people trust us and share things with us in confidence. The information they've entrusted to us makes them vulnerable, and we should never use that knowledge to harm them. In other words, we don't attack people when their backs are turned. We respect their trust and remain loyal keepers of any secrets they share with us.

Even when someone does something really offensive and hurtful, we are bound by honor and chivalry not to use private knowledge to inflict pain. Of course, if we are armed with sensitive information, we may be tempted to inflict the same kind of pain someone has inflicted on us. At times revenge can sound pretty appealing, even justified. But that's not how a follower of Jesus should respond, and it's not the example he set for us.

If you believe what the New Testament says, Jesus had scandalous information on *every* person he ever met, but the only time that he "spilled the beans" was with the woman at the well. "It's true you're not married—but you've had five husbands and the guy you're living with now is not your husband,"[1] he basically said. But notice that Jesus shared this with the woman herself *in private*, not in front of the whole village or even in front of his disciples. Jesus was the ultimate example of chivalry. We need to follow his lead and commit to never using inside information to hurt others.

SAVE THE DRAMA

Have you ever been in a seemingly insignificant conversation when the other person starts telling you about an argument he or she had? Before you know it, you're buried in drama. You're learning details you probably shouldn't know—or you're listening as your friend unloads negative feelings about someone else.

When you find yourself in this situation, you have the opportunity to do one of three things:

1. Place your hand on the knife being driven into someone's back and plunge it in even deeper by participating in the discussion.

2. Say nothing, but allow the gossip and backstabbing to continue, while the victim is unaware of the attack.

3. Speak up and put a stop to the gossip. Perhaps you can correct the misinformation or defend the character of the person being maligned. You might not even know whether the comments are true, but that isn't the point. You have the option of ending the attack. After all, if it were you being dissed, wouldn't you want someone to have your back?

In these situations, you have only a moment to decide what to do. Make the chivalrous choice. Stop the gossip before it does real damage.

When friends speak to each other, there is an implied level of trust. This is true even when friends speak poorly about someone else—their word is trusted. This is one of the dangers in gossiping. Suppose you say something to a good friend about someone else. You two begin connecting the dots and drawing conclusions that may or may not be true about another person. Then one of you shares your conclusions with another friend. They share it with someone else. Pretty soon, what began as a casual comment grows into an amalgamated picture of the person you're gossiping about. This picture—a myth—spreads, and before long, you've potentially ruined someone's reputation.

"WELL, IT'S TRUE"

My friends know I can be very sarcastic. In the past, that has been something I prided myself on. Not so much anymore. The problem comes when a comment meant in good fun crosses the line into hurtful. It can be hard to know the difference.

I still think it's okay to mess with your friends, to tell jokes and kid around. I like being thought of as clever or funny. My family is full of wordsmiths, and I value wit. But I know that, in some cases, I have hurt people's feelings with my sarcasm.

Why is sarcasm hard to control at times, and why do some people seem to use it so frequently? I think it's because sarcasm is the result of feeling uncomfortable or threatened. It often comes from trying to fill empty, awkward space in a conversation. To compensate, we try to be funny by making a joke about someone else—and can potentially cause hurt feelings. This can become a bad habit that is difficult to rein in.

How do we know when to remain silent if we have an urge to make a sarcastic comment? Here are three pretty safe rules in relation to that. As chivalrous people, we should avoid sarcasm that

weaves in a thread of truth that may be funny but is
    also hurtful,
is about someone's flaw or fault, or
is about how someone is different or doesn't fit in.

How would you feel if it were you, your best friend, or a family member who was the topic of this sarcastic remark? If you wouldn't want it said about them, don't say it about anyone else. That's a good barometer when it comes to living the chivalrous life.

Don't get me wrong: It is okay to be funny. It is okay to be ironic. Teasing someone usually means that you have a relationship with that person, that you know each other. Sarcasm could be either ammunition in a verbal gun—something to hurt them with—or it could be a lighthearted joke between friends. We just have to be careful. Just because something is true, doesn't mean we have to say it. Just because it's funny doesn't mean it's fair.

FACE-TO-FACE

To avoid misunderstandings, we need to evaluate not only what we say but the method we use to say it. Part of maturing is knowing when and how to communicate with people. When is a quick text the best option? When do they really need to hear our voice? When should we talk face-to-face?

In my experience, the more important the topic, the less technology you should use to discuss it. If there's a big decision to be made, a sensitive item for discussion, or the chance of mis- understanding, you should talk face-to-face. If it's consequential, takes time, is about a work-related issue, or brings about serious change, the discussion should be done in person. If it's a subject of great weight—personal or professional—you should take it to the other person directly. This is not the time for a text.

Breakups, criticism, or asking someone out on a date should be done face-to-face, or at least voice to voice—*not* through texts. If it's anything important, look the person in the eye. If you've heard a rumor or if you have reason to doubt a friend, go to him or her and talk it over in person.

Here's an example of what I mean: I knew a guy named Ron who said something that really bothered me. I don't get offended easily when it comes to personal attacks, but in this case I perceived his comments as racist. Ron is a white guy, which made it easier for me to assume a negative meaning in his words. I didn't think what he said was funny, and I told him so. Our conversation ended awkwardly.

I told someone else that I was annoyed by what had happened, even alluding to the fact that Ron's remark was the type that could start a fistfight. That was the wrong thing for me to do; I should have left it alone or gone to Ron in person if I wanted to discuss the issue further. Word got around a little bit, and Ron came back to me and expressed regret for what he'd said. It was an extremely humble apology. Instead of texting me or sending me a Facebook message, he actually came to me, looked me in the eye, and apologized. I forgave him. In that situation where I had failed, Ron did the right thing.

The next time you have to choose between a face-to-face meeting, a phone call, or a text, ask yourself these questions: Is it a difficult discussion? Could it be misinterpreted? Is it something you've been putting off? If the answer is yes, it's probably best to meet one-on-one and look the person in the eye.

AT THE HEART OF IT

Criticism seems to be our culture's favorite hobby. But as chivalrous people, we need to go against the mainstream. Think long and hard before criticizing anyone. How we offer helpful criticism is also important; we must earn the right to tell someone something tough, and we must be in a position to do so in love. It's helpful to ask ourselves, *What's the goal?* We need to be honest with ourselves and know where our motivation stands. Are we just trying to sound smart or look better than others? Are we hoping to get back at them or put them in their place? Would we feel justified in telling them something difficult? Are we really trying to help them and build them up?

Another approach is to imagine how we would feel receiving that criticism. *If the situation were reversed, would I want them to say the same thing to me?* It's pretty simple, guys: it's the Golden Rule. This is an ancient piece of wisdom, but it still rings true today. It's in the Torah as, "Love your neighbor as yourself. I am the Lord."[2] Years later, Confucius reiterated the same idea: "Do not inflict on others what you yourself would not wish done to you."[3] And Jesus taught his followers, "Do to others whatever you would like them to do to you."[4]

Before you criticize, take an extra second or two and ask yourself the question, *Does this violate that simple Golden Rule?* Meditate on this. Think on it. Examine your life, your heart, and your mind, and look at the times when you have not done this. Allow yourself to feel convicted, and then do better next time. Don't only do better—get better.

In order to make things right, we have to recognize that something is wrong and identify it clearly. If we wish to change something in others, if we want them to see a need for change in the world, we have to recognize fractures in our own souls. We have to examine the hurting in ourselves and in the world. We have to know that something is wrong. And we cannot, under any circumstance, run from the necessary pain of growth, improvement, and learning to love. This is the way of chivalry.

Once when Jesus was talking to some pompous religious people, they asked him, "Why don't your disciples wash their hands before they eat? It's an ancient custom, and they are breaking God's law!"

What was Jesus' response? "It's not what goes into your mouth that defiles you; you are defiled by the words that come out of your mouth."

Then Jesus' disciples came to him and asked, "Do you realize you offended the Pharisees by what you just said?"

Jesus replied that the way the Pharisees led their followers was like one blind man trying to lead another blind man to safety—they would both end up in a ditch.[5]

> Then Peter said to Jesus, "Explain to us the parable that says people aren't defiled by what they eat."
> "Don't you understand yet?" Jesus asked. "Anything you eat passes through the stomach and then goes into the sewer. But the words you speak come from the heart—that's what defiles you. For from the heart come evil thoughts, murder, adultery, all sexual immorality, theft, lying, and slander. These are what defile you. Eating with unwashed hands will never defile you."[6]

What's important is what is in my heart, and what I want in my heart is a love for people and a desire to honor them.

Even more than what we do is what we think of doing. What consumes our thoughts, what feelings we allow to take hold—those are what define us. Out of the overflow of our hearts our mouths speak.[7] Who we are and what our hearts hold will be shown in the words we say.

CHALLENGE

We have all met people whose only conversational interest seems to be talking about other people. They love to gossip about who's in a relationship, who doesn't like someone else, or who looks bad. If you're around these people for even a short time, you're going to hear commentary about someone who is not there. These conversations are often real-life tabloids, minus the red-carpet photos.

Although we instantly recognize this trait in other people, sometimes it's easy to overlook in ourselves. What about you? Is talking about others a habit? Have you ever tried to go a full week—or maybe just a day—without saying something about another person behind his or her back? If even one day is a challenge, then try to go an afternoon without sneaking in a few words of minor scandal.

When we're talking with friends, it's easy to get careless, to just talk and talk without thinking about what we're saying. But we *should* be careful about what we say—especially when our emotions are high. One indicator that we need to watch our words is indignation rising in our chests. When we feel frustrated, angry, or confused, we often say things we don't mean. Or we say things that we mean in the most hurtful way possible; that's usually the stuff that we've held on to for a long time and that we should have communicated at another time, in another way. At least then we're saying something to the person's face and not behind his or her back. Just because it's true doesn't justify saying something mean.

What if we turned this whole concept on its head? Why don't we pledge to bless others and not to curse them? I don't mean "curse" as in swearing or using foul language. (That's another topic.) But what if, instead of gossiping about people's problems, we tried to say positive things about them when they're not around? *Especially* people we may not particularly *like*. As my mom says, "If you find that you're jealous of people, try celebrating their success and saying something good about them."

Here's your chance to try this out. The next time you're watching *American Idol* or some other performance show on

TV, or when your friends start bashing a celebrity, make an effort to say something nice about that person. If you declined to say negative things about the performer on TV, or if you changed the subject when somebody started to criticize a person you don't even know, how much easier would it be to stop saying negative things about people you see day-to-day? (The answer is "Much easier." I'll give you that one.)

In reality, this takes practice. It really is hard sometimes, especially when we know people who just seem mean or annoying. It would serve them right to have a whole campus, office, or church full of people talking about them behind their backs. It would feel pretty sweet to give them what they deserve.

> **"We should be too big to take offense and too noble to give it."**
>
> ABRAHAM LINCOLN

We need to follow the example of the knights of old. To them, another person's behavior did not dictate the civility of their response. Even more so with my hero, Jesus of Nazareth. He taught me to offer more of myself when someone insults me in the worst way. That whole thing about turning the other cheek when someone hits you in the face? That was his idea.[8] And it's possibly even more extreme than that. To hit you on the right cheek, someone would have to use their left hand—the "unclean" hand. Back in the day, where Jesus came from, that hand would not have been used for anything good. People used the left hand to clean themselves in the bathroom. Get the picture? If someone smacked you with that hand, it was considered the worst kind of insult possible.

Chivalry is a completely crazy standard. How can Jesus expect people to put up with stuff like that? It doesn't make sense. But in a way, this makes it easier because we don't have to treat people differently based on how nice they are to us. Even if they slap us with the unclean hand, our job is still to love and respect them, to return their curses with blessings.

The behavior of others is not our responsibility. Chivalry isn't even so much about our own behavior as it is about what's in our minds and hearts and how that affects the way we live— and it must.

We will not gossip about people. We will be kind.

And we will never attack from behind.

I WILL PRACTICE
SELF-CONTROL &
SELFLESSNESS.

"We always pay dearly for chasing after what is cheap."

ALEKSANDR I. SOLZHENITSYN

WHAT YOU DO OR DON'T DO

Self-control is not about what you shouldn't do. It is about what you *should* do. You *should* exercise restraint. You *should* think before you act.

Consider, for example, romantic relationships. Too often, we talk about what young Christian couples *shouldn't* do together. We categorize the expressions of physical intimacy, separating them into different levels. Petting: light and heavy. Kissing: cheek, lips, tongue. I took sex ed at a Christian high school in Georgia. The teachers had us talking through all of this stuff. And then they told us not to do any of it because then we'd end up having sex—which is something you should not do before marriage.

For the record, I agree with the idea that you should be celibate until marriage, and if marriage isn't for you, then stay celibate. I'm down with that. That's great. Save sex for marriage, for the one person you're willing to commit to for life.

But instead of focusing on how we *should* have self-control, we focus on what not to do. I think that's the wrong emphasis.

Self-control is its own action, not merely an avoidance of other actions. It seems counterintuitive to focus on what we don't want to do, rather than concentrating on the things we should be doing. Baseball players focus on making contact with the ball—not striking out. Tightrope walkers look ahead—not down at the ground. The same principle applies to self-control. Focusing on what we want to avoid only diverts our minds from what we want to do or be. We should focus our minds on good things, on our goals.

Here's an idea: practice self-control in the small things, the ordinary things. Self-control is more of a choice to accept the best thing rather than to resist the wrong thing. Trying to get in shape? It takes discipline and willpower to eat well and work out. But it's less about avoiding dessert and more about doing what's best for your body every day.

The same concept is particularly important in romantic relationships. So much in our culture points to the thrill of sexual gratification that it can seem like all the world is obsessed with sex. This includes those who believe in gratifying all impulses and desires *and* those who feel that God is pleased with us when we control ourselves and our urges. Everyone seems unable to stop thinking and talking about sex, temptation, lust, and the reasons we should or should not pursue every sexual desire.

Sexual attraction and impulse are incredibly powerful forces. That's why I'm taking so much time in this chapter to address them. But I've also talked with guys my age who have said, "I never had a problem with that type of temptation until my youth leader started talking about how to deal with sexual desires."

Did you get that? For many of us, thinking and talking about what we should *not* do could be the very fuel on the fire that drives us in that direction, not away from it. If someone tells you over and over not to think about cowboy hats, you're going to start thinking about cowboy hats.

Instead of telling us not to have certain thoughts, what if someone said, "Here's what I want you to think about: the type of person you want to be and the specific types of relationships you want to have."

What if, instead of drawing the boundaries of physical intimacy, we declare to ourselves and to our friends what we *do* want the relationship to be? It might sound something like this: "I want to honor the person I'm dating and consider him or her more important than myself. I believe the future well-being of our relationship—whether it's a short-term dating relationship or a lifelong marriage—is more important than the urges I'm feeling right now. I want to prove to others, to my culture, that relationships don't have to be defined by sexual encounters and conquests, but can be defined by how people treat each other with sacrificial love, dignity, and respect."

Please forgive me for being blunt here, but when we start drawing lines about what we will or won't do physically with another person, when we apply those lines to the bodies of the people we're dating, aren't we basically making those people a collection of body parts rather than unique, highly significant individuals?

REGRETS—AND NO REGRETS

I want to live without regrets. I want you to live without regrets, too, my friend, especially regrets over your relationships. I'm not talking about a lack of regret that comes from saying "You only live once" and then choosing to do whatever you feel like doing. Those are actually a recipe for guilt and disappointment. Don't fall into their trap either. But I want you to avoid regrets by having a heart that longs for the good of yourself and others so much that you wouldn't want to do anything to hurt someone else or to compromise your morals.

Sure, it feels good to look in people's eyes and see that they are attracted to you. But saying or doing things you'll regret is not worth the short-term enjoyment or pleasure. Because afterward, you're left with two choices: drowning out the sound of your own guilt and regret (which is dangerous and desensitizes your heart) or apologizing to those you have hurt. Even after "making things better" with people you have hurt, you can never take back what you said or did. You can't erase people's thoughts or memories about you, and you can't really forget either.

I'm speaking from experience. I've gone through my own relational heartache, including a serious breakup. In the aftermath, I took the first path, questioning and trying to drown everything out. It was awful. I tried for the life of me to recover. I felt betrayed and upset and crushed with how everything ended. When you go through the cutting of strong ties and the burning of oft-frequented bridges, things aren't the same. They can't be the same.

As author William Arthur Ward said, "We can become bitter or better; upset or understanding; hostile or humble; furious or forgiving."[1] After my breakup, I became bitter. I acted insensitively and stupidly.

I consumed entertainment that had few redemptive qualities just for shock value. I'm not a legalist; it's not like I only listen to Christian bands or only read Christian books. But I began listening to stuff that had nothing good, true, or beautiful in it. It was just anger, hate, and volume—at high decibels. I acted as though it was cool not to care about the things that mattered most. I was playing a role, pretending to be cool and detached. And it really stunk. I was not happy. I hurt people's feelings. I compromised. I said and did whatever I felt like saying and doing.

I tried to drown out my own regret and self-doubt by turning up the volume of increasingly shocking and offensive content. When that stopped working, I started treating people differently, brashly. I hurt people's feelings.

I hung out with only two friends during that short period—one guy and one girl. I ended up leading the girl on and treating her poorly. And I was a bad influence on the guy, someone who was supposed to be like my brother.

I ended up breaking contact with those two friends. Yet, there was still hurt. I felt like I had been a different person with them—a negative person susceptible to suggestions and encouragement to do things I wouldn't normally do. And I had to put that behind me. I didn't want them to suffer more because of me. It never feels good to cut ties.

During this period of my life, I had what some call "diarrhea of the mouth." I said whatever came to mind, bad language and rude humor included. I compromised. I went with the flow rather than exerting some effort to do what I knew was right, and the flow took me to places I don't want to revisit. Friendships—not just mine—were severed.

I was trying to live a life without consequences. In reality, I made poor choices and hurt feelings and came close to endangering some friends one night when a few stupid online comments turned into a face-to-face confrontation.

It was then that I realized the truth I had been ignoring: Everything has consequences. Everything counts.

There is no such thing as "just a movie." "Just a song." "Just words." "Just a kiss." Nothing is trivial. Everything has repercussions.

Although I've gotten my act together a lot since then, I still regret the bad choices I made, the ways I hurt people. Those people might find it ironic that I'm writing this book. I'm still disappointed in myself. But now I know what I want to do differently. I want self-control. It's not natural—human nature is to put ourselves first, to get more, to be like everyone else. But we're called to a higher standard. As chivalrous people, we're called to embrace self-control.

My behavior should reflect the person I say I serve. I say I follow Jesus. This life I want to live, reflecting this person, requires supernatural strength and fruit in my life that can come only from my Creator.

POWER UNDER CONTROL

My dad has told me that: "True manliness is power under control."

That's not exactly the way men are portrayed today. The popular, stereotypical, modern view of gender roles paints a different picture of a "man's man," or a real "blokey bloke," as some would say. Guys are expected to be emotionally insensitive, physically strong, mentally tough, and always ready (or willing) to fight.

The opposite could be said about true womanhood. Women are expected to be beautiful and sensitive, to be aware of their bodies and to use their femininity to get what they want—learning how to turn heads and mess with them.

Whether you're a guy or a girl, you have power. We all do. The question is, how are we using it? Are the portrayals I mentioned good uses of our power? Is this really what it means to be a man or a woman?

I believe that you and I are capable of a whole lot, for good and for bad. But if we don't live out self-control and selflessness, we can easily fall into the trap of abusing our power. To avoid this, let's look at some keys to exercising discipline over our natural impulses.

Most people who've grown up going to a Christian church can name the various "fruit of the Spirit." You might even know the song for it. These fruits are the ways our faith should be visible in our lives:

> The fruit of the Spirit is love, joy, peace, forbearance
> [patience], kindness, goodness, faithfulness, gentleness
> and self-control.
>
> GALATIANS 5:22-23, NIV

Fruits, huh? So . . . I'm a tree.

This isn't the first or only time in the Bible that people are compared to plants and their behavior is described as fruit. There are a couple of verses of poetry from the Psalms that refer to this same idea:

> Oh, the joys of those who do not
>   follow the advice of the wicked,
>   or stand around with sinners,
>   or join in with mockers.
> But they delight in the law of the LORD,
>   meditating on it day and night.
> They are like trees planted along the riverbank,
>   bearing fruit each season.
>   Their leaves never wither,
>   and they prosper in all they do.
>
> PSALM 1:1-3

This makes sense to me. Put good into your lifestyle, and you'll get good out. If you're watered, you'll flourish. If you are planted in a great place, with fertile soil and an ideal climate, you'll produce fruit in season and prosper in all you do—maybe not financially, but in the ways that matter most.

Matthew, one of Jesus' first followers, quotes Jesus as saying, "By their fruit you will recognize them. Do people pick grapes from thornbushes, or figs from thistles? Likewise, every good tree bears good fruit, but a bad tree bears bad fruit. A good tree cannot bear bad fruit, and a bad tree cannot bear good fruit."[2]

We should be able to recognize the work of God in people by looking at their behavior. If we are trying to live in a way that reflects the teachings in the Bible, and if we have a real relationship with this guy named Jesus, these are the traits we will portray—or the fruit we'll be producing—on a regular basis:

love,
joy,
peace,
patience,
kindness,
goodness,
faithfulness,
gentleness,
and . . .
self-control.

If you're a Christian and believe the Bible, you know that the Holy Spirit of God actually lives inside of you (which is strange and cool). His influence in our lives is what empowers us to display these character traits. According to this passage, if we're trees fed by God's Spirit, we'll display several clear markings—including self-control. Yep, it's one of the top nine things that we (and others around us) should see in our lives if we claim to be followers of Jesus.

I asked some of my friends what they know about self-control. The first, almost instinctive response was a sarcastic, "Oh, I'm really great at that. You should definitely ask me about it."

So point one about self-control: I'm bad at it. (And if you're honest, you'll probably admit you struggle with it too.)

I think we can pretty easily define and talk about improving on the other eight traits. But why does self-control evade us so often? Part of it could be a cultural thing. Self-control is not a quality that our society embraces. It might be different if you don't live in a Western culture. But in my backyard, I find that . . .

We are impulsive.

We want what we want, when we want it. And we can pretty much have it.

The people who are the most powerful get what they want, when they want it. As much of it as they want.

And instead of acknowledging this as a psychological issue, we think it's power. "Hey, I've earned it," we say. "Why not indulge?"

We feel a little hungry, so we get a snack whenever we want one.

We get bored, so we immediately access something entertaining. (Confession: I just wasted an hour or two watching videos on YouTube when I should have been writing a chapter on self-control.)

Think of self-control as a muscle; we have to stretch it to practice using it if it's going to do us any good. Small acts of self-denial may help build the discipline to resist temptation when something more consequential comes up.

I don't know who said it first, but the statement is at least decades old: "Character is who you are when no one is looking." That speaks directly to the topic of self-control. If no one is watching you or monitoring your behavior, if you can do anything you want—well, what do you do? Who are you? What kind of self-control do you exercise?

If you had the resources and time to always do whatever you wanted, who would you become? Would you impose boundaries and guidelines on yourself, or would you remove all constraints?

There's a *Calvin and Hobbes* comic that brings this to life. In case you don't know, Calvin is a wild, spiky-haired, six-year-old boy who is often insightful beyond his years, and Hobbes is his stuffed toy tiger who gives pretty good advice, except when it comes to math. In this comic strip, Calvin and Hobbes are leaning against a tree when Calvin wonders aloud whether money, power, or fame is the true secret to happiness. Then Calvin says, "*I'd* choose money. If you have enough money, you can *buy* power and fame. That way you'd have it all and be *really* happy!"

The next thing Calvin says is the part that really strikes me: "Happiness is being famous for your financial ability to indulge in every kind of excess."[3]

> **"Give love to the ones who can't love at all.**
>
> **Give hope to the ones who got no hope at all.**
>
> **Stand up for the ones who can't stand at all."**
>
> JON FOREMAN, "INSTEAD OF A SHOW"

The creator of the comic, Bill Watterson, is delivering a pretty deep commentary on our culture. He uses the ironic statement of a child to point out the glaring error of a philosophy—Calvin says he wants money and power so he can crush people. His wish, unrestrained by self-control, is to be able to do whatever he wants, without regard to how it affects others.

Obviously, a cartoon character is not our example for how to live our lives. But something as small as a comic strip can hold a mirror to how our culture defines power and force us to face it. What you do with the knowledge of this unfavorable reflection is your decision.

GIVING IN

I enjoy sitting around with friends over a cup of coffee and talking about big ideas and little mundane things, about our future plans and dreams—about *life* and how we should live it. As a Christian, I believe there are things I should avoid doing. Not everything I desire or everything I want to do is the best for me—you know, inclinations toward doing things that are harmful to me or someone else. This can be tricky because not everyone has the same areas of weakness. What might be okay for you might not be okay for me, and vice versa. There are choices people make about certain behaviors that are totally fine for them, but I'm better off choosing differently. These are instances where I will restrict my freedom and use self-control, not to appear better than anyone else but because those behaviors don't benefit me.

Some of my friends would say that we should never resist a natural impulse. If you feel like doing something, you should do it. Doing anything other than giving in to an impulse is harmful to you spiritually and mentally. That's their logic.

I have also heard this argument: "We can't be so arrogant as to assume that we could possibly know the best way to do something. This includes the way to enlightenment, the way to salvation. I can't tell someone what to believe. In the same way, I can't tell someone how to act. If a friend of mine is doing something that he thinks is right, I shouldn't stop him. If I'm doing what *I* think is right, you have no right to try to stop me, even if you don't agree with it."

My response: "What if I have a friend whom I love a lot. And what if this friend is doing something that is harming him, but he has no problem with it. For the sake of argument, let's say this friend really likes cocaine. He has it for breakfast. But I see that it's messing him up, changing his personality, causing him to make bad decisions that will eventually hurt him and others. I believe it would be irresponsible and cruel *not* to say something to help him see the dangers of what he's doing. If I really care about him, I'm compelled to help him. What you're saying sounds really cool and existential and all that. But when it comes to caring about a friend of mine, I can't just sit back and let him hurt himself or someone else."

I understand where people might be coming from when they say we should allow our minds and hearts to guide us. Disney movies—that's where this stuff comes from. I'm kidding, of course. But we *have* been raised on this idea. It's a theme we've heard in countless films. Wasn't it Pinocchio's friend Jiminy Cricket who said, "Always let your conscience be your guide"? That sounds harmless, right? Just follow your heart—your own inner moral compass—and you can't go wrong.

But I know my own heart. I know my own thoughts, when

I'm operating by my own rules. The truth is, I'm a selfish pig. When left to my own devices, I really mess things up.

If I did not practice self-control, if I acted on all of my impulses, I would hurt a lot of people—maybe not physically, but definitely emotionally. I would make foolish decisions and probably waste some great opportunities. And if my friends saw me doing that, I wouldn't want them to let me ruin my life. I'd want them to step in and warn me. So if I see people I love hurting themselves or someone else, I feel it is my responsibility to do what I can to stop or prevent further pain. A lack of self-control leads to many bad results. Letting someone do something stupid isn't showing compassion; it's showing you couldn't care less.

PRACTICE, PRACTICE, PRACTICE

As chivalrous people, we need to rehearse and practice self-control in the small things so we won't fail in the big things.

Decline is the natural state of humankind. Our nature is like water in its liquid state. Always flowing, even rushing, down the path of least resistance. On average, we do what is easiest.

Transcending, rising above—that is different. That is countercultural.

When I talk about transcendence, I don't mean what happens when you go inside of yourself and focus on your emotions. Transcendence is not the state of having traveled inward to the point of losing contact with the outside world. It's much more practical than that. Transcendence is when a person rises above his or her nature. When practice has made it easier to resist natural impulses. This is when self-control becomes a reflex and human nature takes a lower position on the totem pole. Transcendence is a supernatural existence, empowered by the Holy Spirit.

I want to live a contemplative life. Hiding in plain sight but still being in the world. Mixed up with everyone else, yet so different from the norm. It's not about being special or better than anyone. I want to be better than myself. I want to listen to things I can't hear with my ears. I want to *not* follow my first impulses. I want to be disciplined and exhibit abnormal self-control. I want to appreciate and enjoy the beauty around me. And I want to love people for who they are, not for how they look or for what they can give me.

I want to be chivalrous. And I want you to join me.

SELF-SACRIFICE AND BEING OTHERS-FOCUSED

As I've said before, this is not intended to be a relationship book. I have a lot to learn in that area and am by no means an expert. But one aspect of self-control that is important in relationships is putting others ahead of ourselves. If we could master the art of self-sacrifice as a part of our growing self-control, people would see an amazing difference in all types of our relationships: parent-child, best friends, boss-employee, teacher-student. People might not recognize us. But they would all be blessed by the transformation.

Self-control in relationships should be what we are headed toward, not what we are running from. When you're on a road trip, your GPS doesn't say, "Don't turn left at the next street. Go five miles, and your destination will not be ahead on your right." No, it tells you exactly where you *should* turn. Are you getting this? Self-control should tell us where to go and what to do. It's not about how we won't engage in certain types of sexual activity, or how we won't watch certain movies, or how we won't indulge our every desire. It's about what we want to do with our lives and where we want to be, both in our individual lives and mutually in our relationships.

In my short life, I have learned a little about love—what it does and doesn't do. What I've determined is that an obsession with what we want only breeds selfishness. But when we focus on what's best for someone else, love blossoms into sacrifice.

When you truly love someone, you are willing to do anything for that person. You will sacrifice your time, money, comfort—anything—for the object of your love. The ultimate expression of love is being willing to die for another, if it comes to that. If you love someone, that person's life becomes more valuable than your own. Essentially, love is all about sacrifice. If you love someone, you will give it all away for the sake of the one you love. Sometimes, this may even mean sacrificing your relationship with that person for his or her own good. Do you see where this is going?

Once a very wise man was faced with a difficult situation. Two women stood before him with just one baby. Each claimed that the child was her own. The man said, "Cut the baby in two and give half to each woman." Our initial reaction is one of horror, but look what happens next. The first woman said, "All right, he will be neither yours nor mine." But the second woman said, "No! Just give the child to her. Don't kill him!" So the wise man gave the child to the woman who wanted him to live, knowing that she must be his mother.[4] Her love was evident in her self-sacrifice. The fact that the mother cared more about her baby than she did about herself allowed her to give him up—even though she loved him more than life itself.

Self-sacrifice and self-control go hand in hand. Both are signs of real love. You can't forfeit your own desires for the sake of someone you love without exercising a hefty amount of self-control. But the opposite is also true. Selfishness and a lack of self-control result in a lot of hurt—for you and the people you love.

MY WORST ENEMY

There are a lot of "self" phrases that wreck people's lives, or at least cause them heartache that could be avoided. We've already covered self-control and selfishness, but there's one last "self" phrase that I want to address. It springs out of pride, just like the other two.

We often think of pride or arrogance in connection with people who are good-looking or talented and obviously know it. These people seem to strut or swagger in time to internal theme music, and they treat others poorly because they think they're better. Those people are pretty hard to miss. If that's you, stop it; you're not all that.

But there's another kind of pride that is more subversive, more insidious. It's called self-consciousness. This is something I have struggled with my whole life. I've often felt insecure about my appearance and my behavior, worrying how I sound to people, how I present myself, how they're going to receive me. People who are self-conscious are focused on their own faults and flaws (or what they perceive their flaws to be). They become experts at magnifying their own problems and worries, fixating on what they think makes them ugly or awkward or unacceptable. If you struggle with this like I do, you know how miserable it can be.

There's another problem with this self-conscious mind-set: when we obsess over how we look and feel, we put ourselves first and others second. We become overly sensitive and attuned to negative aspects of ourselves. This is a high form of pride, and it keeps us from focusing on the needs and hurts of other people. Without realizing it, we can allow ourselves to become so distracted by our own issues that we end up ignoring or neglecting ways we can serve and help those around us.

How can we keep our self-consciousness from limiting us? I have found that the best way to stop focusing on myself is to try to make other people feel comfortable or cared for. Even though I often feel as though I'm the most awkward person in the room, I try to find someone else who looks nervous or doesn't have anyone to talk to. I'm an introvert, but I've practiced being a people person. And practice, at the very least, makes acceptable (since perfection is a myth).

All in all, it's about getting outside of ourselves, moving the spotlight away from us and onto someone else. We are not necessarily the stars of our own stories, and we are certainly not the center of the universe. Through selfishness, self-consciousness, and a lack of self-control, we block ourselves from being able to focus on others and make them feel important; in fact, doing more harm than good. As humans, it is our nature to look out for number one. But the purpose of this quest is to transcend our nature, to make others number one.

In our journey toward chivalry, self-control grows while self-indulgence, selfishness, and self-consciousness shrink back and submit.

IV

I WILL
RESPECT
LIFE AND
FREEDOM.

"To be free is not merely to cast off one's chains, but to live in a way that respects and enhances the freedom of others."

NELSON MANDELA

PLANTED IN THE MARYLAND SOIL

ON A FRIGID FEBRUARY MORNING in Maryland, 1817, a baby boy was born to a slave woman by the name of Harriet Bailey.

Only forty-one years earlier, the Declaration of Independence had been signed, proclaiming that "all men are created equal." Yet this baby, Frederick Augustus Washington Bailey, was born a slave, considered to be less than a person. Why? Because his skin was a few shades darker than the white plantation owner's.

He had no father. At least none who would claim him. Even though his father was likely Caucasian, Frederick was still black. And he was considered "property."

Frederick's mother, Harriet, worked as a field hand twelve miles from where he was raised by his grandparents. He saw her only during the nighttime, when she would risk her own safety to walk the entire twelve miles on foot and lie beside him to help him sleep.

When Frederick was seven years old, he received word that his mother had died. But young Frederick had barely spent any time with his mother; in fact, he once said that he had never seen her in the daylight. His mother was such a stranger that he felt no loss at her death.

When we think of slavery, don't we most often think about inhumane treatment, backbreaking labor, awful living conditions? Or do we think about being the property of another human being? Do we stop to consider the way slavery tore families apart? Mothers were sold away from their children. Husbands and wives were separated by a quick sale, never to see each other again. Human lives, riven.

But slavery didn't just take people away from their families; it prevented them from having families in the first place.

Frederick was born into bondage, both mentally and physically. Thoughts, emotions, and human connection were all dulled by the system of slavery.

Frederick remembers his master, Captain Anthony, being incredibly cruel. And the overseer, Mr. Plummer, was even worse, always walking around with a cowhide whip and a heavy club.

Frederick continued to grow up in the care of his grandmother, along with several other children. Even though he wasn't forced to work as a child, he was still a slave. He was denied the dignity of being treated like a human being.

At age nine, Frederick was sent to Baltimore to be a playmate for his owner's relative. Frederick was *sent*. Like a parcel. Like a package. He was basically sent to be the pet of another child.

While in Baltimore, Frederick learned to read and write from his new mistress. That is, until her husband stepped in, saying, "Learning would . . . forever unfit him to be a slave. He would at once become unmanageable and of no value to his master."

Frederick refused to be dumbed down. He would sneak peeks into his playmate's books. When he was down at the shipyard, he would trace letters to learn the alphabet. He would also challenge local white boys to writing contests so he could improve his own.

At sixteen, rebellious and confident, he was sent back to his old master's associate, Thomas Auld. A year later, Auld hired him out to Edward Covey for one year. Covey was a farmer infamous for breaking so-called disrespectful slaves.

Frederick was awkward on the farm because he had never

had to work in a field before. He was seldom without a bleeding back, covered in welts the size of a man's finger.

Covey was known for sneaking up on slaves who tried to take a break. After working six months for Covey, Frederick was broken in body, soul, and spirit. However, there was a turning point that made the last six months more bearable than the first. When Covey attacked and began to beat him, Frederick fought back. In his own words, "At this moment—from whence came the spirit I don't know—I resolved to fight; and, suiting my action to the resolution, I seized Covey hard by the throat." After fighting for nearly two hours, Covey let him go. But as Frederick said, "I considered him as getting entirely the worst end of the bargain; for he had drawn no blood from me, but I had from him. The whole six months afterwards, that I spent with Mr. Covey, he never laid the weight of his finger upon me in anger."[1]

Boldness and defiance took the place of submission in Frederick's heart, though it might have gotten him killed. In 1836, he got together with four other slaves and planned a runaway attempt, which was discovered and foiled in advance.

Thomas Auld hired him out again, this time as an apprentice ships' calker back in Baltimore. While there, he made a friend, a free black woman by the name of Anna Murray. She helped him obtain forged papers that declared him a free black sailor. He took a train to New York City and, by doing so, escaped from slavery. Anna followed him, and they were married.

With the help of the famed Underground Railroad, they moved to New Bedford, Massachusetts. There Frederick Bailey changed his last name to Douglass. And so Frederick Douglass was "born."

Douglass went from free state to free state speaking about his experience and became well known for being a man of accessible eloquence and inspiring passion. In 1839, Douglass met William Lloyd Garrison, who published an abolitionist newspaper.

The meeting influenced Frederick to write a book about his experiences.

Narrative of the Life of Frederick Douglass was basically his journal. His personal reflections on what he actually experienced. It's intense and awful and beautiful. And it was extremely successful in its day. (It's still one of my favorite books.)

Frederick wrote more throughout his life and even became an advisor to Abraham Lincoln. By then the American Civil War (or the War Between the States) had already started, and Douglass was advocating for making the emancipation of slaves a part of the Union's cause. Because of the respect that he earned over time, he became an advisor for four United States presidents.

Many of us don't realize what an incredible gift freedom is. It is a gift that transcends currency.

Frederick Douglass freed himself, but he didn't just sit in a rocking chair, sipping iced tea and saying, "Ah, it's good to be a free man."

He spent his freedom on behalf of those who were not free.

How much more, then, should we who were born free fight to free those who cannot free themselves?

LEARNING FROM THE PAST

I once was asked by an older white Christian lady who has her own radio show about what I've done to end modern-day slavery. She asked me, "Now, these slaveholders you are talking about are nothing like the benevolent slaveholders of the South, right?" I felt blood rise to my face like mercury in a thermometer stuck in an oven.

Does Frederick's story sound like benevolence to you? Even at the most basic level, one human owning another human as property is evil. And I don't throw the word *evil* around casually.

Slavery is not solely a political issue, an economic issue, or a spiritual issue, although all of these factors played a part in slavery in the United States. Exploitation and cruelty to humans is not to be excused. Slavery is one of the biggest blemishes on the face of American history, and it led to countless other evils. The fact that people with my skin color thought it was okay to own other people because they had more melanin in their skin is infuriating and completely embarrassing. On this, we must agree.

It's been said that "he who ignores history is destined to repeat it." If we don't want that to happen to us, we must learn from the past.

One of the most important things a chivalrous person can do is learn. About other nations. About other cultures. About the challenges, pains, victories, and joys of other people. And about history.

My friends know I love a good biography—seeing what made someone tick, what motivated him to do good, or even to do wicked things, and how that one person has changed the course of history. Many of the freedom fighters, abolitionists, and human rights workers of our world's past are my heroes. Frederick Douglass is at the top of that list.

When I'm thinking about freedom, I realize that mine really hasn't cost me much. That's why it helps me to get some perspective by learning from people whose freedom cost a great deal, or who fight for the freedom of others. There is so much we can learn from the life of one chivalrous man who overcame the plight of slavery and then became an instrument of freedom and peace for countless others. He did it through the process of telling his story, of educating, of capturing history for all the ages.

If you haven't read *Narrative of the Life of Frederick Douglass*, I strongly recommend it. In fact, I think it could change your life and your perspective on freedom. The timeless language and message make the book seem as though it could have been written today.

One of Douglass's most powerful writings (famous among abolitionists ever since it was published) is a letter he wrote to his slave master. Can you imagine what kind of message you would send to someone who had owned you, mistreated you, rented you out to others, and abused people you cared about?

I am in awe of the way Frederick Douglass chose to communicate with such a man, treating him with dignity and respect he didn't deserve. Douglass didn't become arrogant or feel entitled in his freedom—neither did he become bitter or vindictive over what had been taken from him.

I had the privilege of meeting Mr. Douglass's great-great-great-grandson a few years ago. Kenneth B. Morris has stepped into the legacy of his famous ancestor and is helping bring hope to people enslaved today. It was an honor for me to spend time with a descendant of this great man and to know Mr. Morris is continuing his family's work for justice.

I recently read the piece below from Douglass's writings that sheds light on the role people of faith played in the slave trade:

I love the pure, peaceable, and impartial Christianity of Christ: I therefore hate the corrupt, slaveholding,

women-whipping, cradle-plundering, partial and
hypocritical Christianity of the land. Indeed, I
can see no reason, but the most deceitful one, for
calling the religion of this land Christianity. . . . We
have men-stealers for ministers, women-whippers
for missionaries, and cradle-plunderers for church
members. The man who wields the blood-clotted
cowskin during the week fills the pulpit on Sunday, and
claims to be a minister of the meek and lowly Jesus. . . .
Revivals of religion and revivals in the slave-trade go
hand in hand together. The slave prison and the church
stand near each other. The clanking of fetters and the
rattling of chains in the prison, and the pious psalm
and solemn prayer in the church, may be heard at the
same time. . . . Here we have religion and robbery the
allies of each other—devils dressed in angels' robes, and
hell presenting the semblance of paradise.[2]

My hope is that people of faith would be a voice for freedom
and a voice for the oppressed. That churches would be safe
havens not for oppressors and prejudice but for those who are
mistreated, marginalized, and misunderstood. This passage in
Amos 5 makes a pretty compelling argument:

I can't stand your religious meetings.
    I'm fed up with your conferences and conventions.
I want nothing to do with your religion projects,
    your pretentious slogans and goals.
I'm sick of your fund-raising schemes,
    your public relations and image making.

I've had all I can take of your noisy ego-music.
When was the last time you sang to *me*?
Do you know what I want?
I want justice—oceans of it.
I want fairness—rivers of it.
That's what I want. That's *all* I want.[3]

We were created to live without shackles. But if you're like me, you also probably don't think much about the fact that you're free. I'm guessing that for slaves throughout history and in the modern-day world, the fact that they aren't free is likely at the front of their minds every day. Maybe it would be a good idea to mull over this idea that what we take for granted—our freedom—isn't a given for others. How will we invest ours? I want to make something amazing out of this gift I have, this gift of freedom.

SPIRITUAL FREEDOM

It's hard to talk about spiritual freedom without sounding heavy-handed or preachy, or repeating things that churchgoers have heard countless times before. It's easy to try to put spiritual statements into religious language, but I have to admit, I'm still figuring this out. Honestly, the idea of spiritual freedom—or as many Christians call it, freedom in Christ—is awkward for me to talk about, because it sounds kind of weird. I'll just talk about what Jesus' freedom means to me. Let's look at this chunk of the Bible from Paul's writings:

All that passing laws against sin did was produce more lawbreakers. But sin didn't, and doesn't, have a chance in competition with the aggressive forgiveness we call *grace*. When it's sin versus grace, grace wins hands down. All sin can do is threaten us with death, and that's the end of it. Grace, because God is putting everything together again through the Messiah, invites us into life—a life that goes on and on and on, world without end.[4]

In short, God's grace is endless. Which begs the question:

So what do we do? Keep on sinning so God can keep on forgiving? I should hope not! If we've left the country where sin is sovereign, how can we still live in our old house there? Or didn't you realize we packed up and left there for good? That is what happened in baptism. When we went under the water, we left the old country of sin behind; when we came up out of the water, we entered into the new country of grace— a new life in a new land![5]

We are free! Free to live however we want. But how, then, *should* we live?

Since we're out from under the old tyranny, does that mean we can live any old way we want? Since we're free in the freedom of God, can we do anything that comes to mind? Hardly. You know well enough from your own experience that there are some acts of so-called freedom that destroy freedom. Offer yourselves to sin, for instance, and it's your last free act. But offer yourselves to the ways of God and the freedom never quits. All your lives you've let sin tell you what to do. But thank God you've started listening to a new master, one whose commands set you free to live openly in *his* freedom![6]

I've been in dark places before. I'm not talking about alleys or windowless rooms or places where poverty is rampant and you can see hunger on the faces of people around you, although I've been to some of those places too. The specific place I'm referring to is a side of myself that, in retrospect, I hate. I've talked about this a bit in the rest of the book, specifically the self-control chapter. I was in quite a bit of emotional turmoil—torment, even. I did (almost) whatever I felt like doing, but I felt constricted and trapped. I don't want to freak anyone out, but I'm serious when I say that I felt actual peace and freedom, like I could breathe more clearly, when I gave up on *trying* so hard to act careless and free. I found freedom in putting boundaries around myself. In giving up my anything-goes attitude. In accepting that I could choose to try to be as "free" as I wanted, but that while everything is possible—permissible, even—not everything is beneficial.[7] *Especially* for leaders.

> **"The word which God has written on the brow of every man is hope."**
> VICTOR HUGO, *LES MISÉRABLES*

This is why it is important to recognize and enjoy your own freedom, not by doing whatever you want but by living freely within good boundaries. It's not confining—it's liberating. What is permissible or good for you may not be good for someone else. Perhaps others feel that God has asked them to set different, more restrictive boundaries in their lives because certain decisions are best for them and other choices may be lethal for them. Just because it's okay for you doesn't mean it's okay for everyone. And just because it's off-limits to you doesn't mean it's off-limits to others.

What does it mean to live free—free to restrict some of our "freedoms" for our own absolute best and for the benefit of others?

What does it mean to give up our rights—to understand that in Jesus we really don't have any rights if we are to die to self?

True freedom involves restricting some of our freedoms. That sounds contradictory, but think about it. Freedom means choosing to resist being like everyone else. When it seems like people do whatever they want, we must choose to be different by setting boundaries for ourselves, limits that will help us make wise choices.

I have a friend, a preacher named Judah Smith. One of the most powerful yet practical sermons I've ever heard is his message called "Mistaken Love."[8] In the message, Judah talks about how sometimes people say he isn't free, or that he is legalistic because he has chosen not to do some things that others think are okay. He explains that his love for Jesus compels him to restrict some of his rights—things he may be free to do but that he has chosen not to, so as not to cause anyone else to stumble. Or to steer clear of actions that could cause him problems down the road. He says he never flirts with other women because he loves his wife. He would not want anyone to misinterpret his actions and think he didn't love her. In the same way, he has chosen to restrict some of his actions and behaviors out of a love for Jesus and for others.

What does it mean to give up our rights in order to gain the ability to love others?

It's actually a pretty lofty, metaphysical thought: in giving something up, you could gain something. You could gain true purpose through figuratively dying to your old self. I've heard people say, "But that was the old me" or "I'm a different person now." I hear people talk about how they don't do certain things anymore, things that used to bring them comfort or pleasure or fulfillment. There are some people for whom drinking is not an issue, but there are others who are truly dependent on alcohol. I've heard people who are so proud of themselves because they haven't been drunk in the longest time, and it used to be something that defined them and caused them to be different people. They feel freer without it.

RESPECT FOR LIFE

Newness is something that children experience on a daily basis. When you've been alive for only a few years, you discover a little something new every day. Imagine with me that Adam was scooped out of the dirt, sculpted into the image of a being who is *love,* and had life breathed into his lungs. A man. For the very first time, seeing everything. Creation. In its wildest, most brand-new, perfect form. A child. A baby. In a man's skin. With a fully developed mind to marvel at everything around him to the fullest. To reason with it. To ask, "Why?" Imagine what it would have been like. Sneezing for the first time would have been pretty terrifying. Think about it. It's funny.

Adam got to walk with God. Imagine that! "Let's take a walk in the garden and enjoy the morning dew. Oh, and great job making all of this, by the way!"

Brand-new. Imagine marveling at your own joints and sinew. How everything bends at your will. Your own power and frailty. The ability to create saliva, the urge to blink, to expel waste. The instinctual draw from the top of a mountain. The bottom of a pond. The color of a fruit. The sound of a bird's song. And you walk with the one who knows you best, the one who is madly in love with you *because* this one knows you . . . and that doesn't disqualify you from being loved. And you are fulfilled. You have communion with the one who made you. He speaks to you, and it is the only voice other than your own that you hear. You are free, without limits and burdens of a past. There is no violence. Everything in existence is yours. Yours to name. What you say it is, that it is. And you know no pain or regret.

God, YHWH, looks at you and says, "It is not good for you to be alone. I'm going to make a companion suitable for you."[9] Relationship. Newness. What does it all mean? God puts Adam to sleep, and when he wakes up . . . he sees what he couldn't have known that he wanted. That he even needed.

Even people who don't believe this really happened must acknowledge the world-altering power and beauty of this moment. The first touch from Eve, awakening him. He didn't know he had all this inside of him. They were naked, but they were not ashamed. And it was beautiful.

The Scriptures that I read as a part of my faith say that humans were made in the image of God and placed a little lower than the angels.[10] God had all he needed, but he created life out of nothing. And it was beautiful.

Life is beautiful, but we seem to lack respect for it. Our culture has become calloused and has chosen which lives are worth saving. My friend Shane describes himself as "passionately pro-life." But he continues, saying, "I just have a much more holistic sense of what it means to be for life, knowing that life does not just begin at conception and end at birth, and that if I am going to discourage abortion, I had better be ready to adopt some babies and care for some mothers."[11] I'm definitely with him on this, despite the fact that it's become a point of contention for many and a very politicized issue (even though I think there are very few issues that are innately political; they are mostly personal and interpersonal).

I am for *all* life. I think we need to respect life infinitely more than we do now. Our culture believes that people are sex objects. Or we act as if someone who has a mental or physical disability is less valuable than someone who is "normal." Or we think it's okay when a person who is too old to be "useful" is dehumanized through the system of care and treatment of the elderly. You may read this and react strongly, saying, "I don't think those things!" But for the most part, we behave as if those are the rules we live by even if we don't consciously think that way. We objectify people in the media (both male and female), we call people "retarded" (a reprehensible use of this word that we must remove from our vocabularies) or "morons," and we treat the elderly poorly, either as invisible or as a burden—or as if their aging bodies render them less intelligent.

PEOPLE WE OFTEN DISRESPECT

When we don't respect life, we don't respect the most vulnerable among us. Here are a few examples:

- **Children**—We need to respect children because they are a sign of hope for our future. Even the simplicity in how they view the world is something we can admire. Jesus valued children and his time with them. If he took the time to be with and hear from children, maybe we should take a cue from him. There's an incredible boy who goes by the nickname Kid President, but his name is actually Robbie. He's known for having some great quotes—and some pretty sweet dance moves. One of the wisest things I've heard in the last year came from his nine-year-old mouth: "Stop being boring, saying stuff like, 'I don't like this. Waah.' Say: 'How can I make things better?' If it doesn't make the world better, don't do it."[12] Now, there's a politician I would campaign for.

- **People who serve**—As chivalrous people, we need to have respect for those whom we think are there to serve us. From janitors to busboys, everyone working in a service job deserves a little extra gratitude. Servers at a restaurant are not our *servants*. I've seen people treat waiters and waitresses like trash—like their occupation minimizes their humanity. The service industry models for us how to treat others, how to put their needs first. There are a lot of people who work very hard to serve and help you. Treat them with dignity, show them honor, and respect their lives.

- **The homeless and poor**—Just because someone is homeless doesn't mean we are better than him or her. Some people shout, "Get a job!" when they drive by a homeless person who is waving a sign. (To see the faces and hear the stories of those living on the streets, visit www.invisiblepeople.tv/blog.) Anyone who shouts such ignorant advice to a person without a home is not being chivalrous.

The poor are viewed as worthless to most of the world. So are the elderly, the disabled, the unborn, the sick. But not to us. We are the civil. We are the chivalrous. We see human worth and worthiness where others see only something to mock. We respect life and freedom.

I WILL FIGHT ONLY
FOR THE SAKE OF THOSE
WHO ARE UNABLE TO
DEFEND THEMSELVES,
OR IN THE DEFENSE
OF JUSTICE.

"I WOULD LIKE
TO BE KNOWN AS
A PERSON WHO
IS CONCERNED
ABOUT **FREEDOM** ←
AND **EQUALITY**
AND **JUSTICE** AND
PROSPERITY FOR
→ **ALL PEOPLE.**"

ROSA PARKS

IN DEFENSE OF *ME*

If people realized how easily they could make a difference, they would have a desire to stand for a noble cause. I honestly believe that. Most people want to know that their lives count, that they can do something here and now to help someone else. Most of us think that we're good people and that we'd readily defend someone else who was in immediate danger.

But do our personal lives reflect this? In reality, what or who do we spend most of our time defending? We can see what matters most to us by looking at what we are willing to fight for.

Think about the last argument you had. Think back over the past week and remember what you pushed back on in a conversation. What did you argue about? What was your last disagreement? Seriously. Write it down or shout it out of a window or something.

Hopefully, you had a couple of helpful, civil disputes. Maybe someone made a racist (or otherwise hurtful) comment, and you called them out. Maybe you had a healthy debate with someone about differing beliefs, and nobody was offended and everyone was still friends.

If so, that's great. You are the one percent.

Did your argument match up with what you say you care about? Let me rephrase that: Were you engaging in a battle that was truly important? Unfortunately, much of what we spend our time and energy fighting for is not.

Here's what I mean: I say I'm a Christian (sometimes reluctantly, because fewer and fewer people really understand what this means). I say I care about people who have been marginalized. I say I care about making sure people feel included. Yet I often find myself with my back against the wall, swinging a sword—not defending the oppressed or what is actually right, but defending myself, my opinions, and what I *think* is the right way of doing something.

We must admit that some things *are not important.* Not everything is worth fighting over.

Let me give you another example. I was flipping through the channels one night and stopped on a TV show called *Lockup*, a documentary series about people in prisons around the United States. One guy had been sentenced to life in prison for killing somebody. He'd already been in for a really long time, and it sounded like he had been shuffled around from cell to cell. He told a story of how a young inmate had "disrespected" him during free time when all the prisoners were allowed to socialize. He said he couldn't let someone get away with disrespecting him, so he took action. He got some bleach from the laundry, ran the water from his faucet as hot as he could, mixed them together, and threw it in the kid's face as he walked by.

This guy didn't throw scalding liquid on someone who was beating up a friend of his, or someone who was physically threatening him. He hurt someone who insulted him. You probably wouldn't think of tossing boiling bleach water on someone who disses you. But you can see where this is going, can't you? We humans are often so filled with pride that we get angry and offended by someone's words against us.

In seventh grade I went to a Christian school where we had to wear ties on Wednesdays for chapel. For some reason, on one particular Wednesday we didn't have to wear a tie. But I didn't know that. When I got to school, a kid made fun of me for wearing a tie, pointing, laughing, the whole deal. Frustrated and embarrassed, I pulled my big old binder out of my backpack and beat him over his head with it. Of course, he started crying. I felt really, really bad. I apologized to him an hour later, and we became friends. I was a child, so there's at least a little bit of an excuse for my behavior. And I was the new kid who didn't know his way around and was being made fun of.

Here's another example from the very normal life of Zach Hunter. I'd just started going to a new college. My first night there, I was talking to a group of girls about random things, trying to get to know them, when the topics of gay marriage/gay rights/homosexuality in general came up. These are what many people refer to as hot-button issues: things that get people angry or excited or cause a debate. So, of course, it came up in conversation on my first night at this school.

One girl said that during her first year at a community college near her hometown, her roommate, whom she had just met, told her, "I'm a lesbian, and I have a girlfriend. I just wanted you to know that."

This girl said that she responded by saying, "I do not approve of that. I believe it's wrong, but I'm not going to judge you."

And her roommate reportedly replied, "That's cool, as long as you don't judge me."

I was pretty surprised as she was telling this story.

I told her I believe that, in such situations, the main point for us as Christians is putting people first as individuals—not the morality of practicing a gay lifestyle.

Why don't we make it our first priority to love people? Why don't we learn about them and their lives and earn the right to share with them about ours? If someone told me very personal details right when we met, I hope I would demonstrate love in my reaction, even if I thought that person's behavior was wrong. I hope I would put the person first. I would hope, over the weeks and months, my new friend would hear that I believe in and follow the teachings of a man named Jesus from a couple of thousand years ago. If so, that person would probably assume that whatever I did and however I treated people would be what Jesus would do and how he would treat people. I hope my representation would be a good one.

FOR OR AGAINST?

For the last few decades Christians have developed the reputation of being defined by what we oppose rather than what, or in whom, we believe. I would rather take time to build relationships with people, demonstrate my care and concern for them, and if and when the time is appropriate, ask some questions that might cause us both to think through thoughtful conversation. I would rather earn the right to be heard.

How would you feel on the other side of meeting a new friend or roommate? What if we just met, and I told you, "Hi, I'm Zach, and I think you're wrong to be in that relationship, drink that, smoke that, watch that movie, listen to that music, or say those words"? Wouldn't you want me to get to know who you are and why you believe what you believe? Wouldn't you be more willing to hear something important from me after you've seen me invest in knowing and understanding you as a person, without dismissing you for your habits or practices?

Many of us (Christians) think we should voice our objections if we hear or see something we perceive to be different from our beliefs, or something immoral according to how we interpret the Bible. And we often do this without being asked, without having a relationship that gives our opinion context, without knowing where the other person is coming from.

I was raised by a marketer and a communications professional, so I often ask the question, "What are we leading with?" What I mean by that is, "What are we giving as a first impression?" In other words, "What are we telling people, through our actions and words, the first time we meet them?"

We need to view ourselves as Christ's ambassadors.[1] As representatives of who we say we believe in. As such, we have to put forward what Jesus would lead with. The first thing out of Jesus' mouth was often a question—not a judgment call or an objection.

We cannot afford to lead with hate or what others may perceive as hate. Although we can't control other people's opinions or perceptions, we can (and should) avoid provoking or insulting them. We cannot afford to lead with petty, denominational "Christiany" yet un-Christlike debates. We cannot afford to lead with opinions expressed in a disrespectful way about people we disagree with. And we can't afford to lead with whether or not we think God predestines people to go to hell. All of that is extremely unappealing.

I'm not suggesting that we "make the gospel palatable." What I'm saying is that we must not lead with the most offensive of our own opinions about what the Bible means. If we lead with our most controversial and possibly inflammatory viewpoints, we lose credibility and shut down the conversation, slamming the door for further, winsome discussion.

As chivalrous ambassadors of Jesus, we *can* put forward the most scandalous aspects of what we call "the Good News." Things like the unconditional love of Christ, extended to you by a stranger—not just Jesus, but also true followers of his. The shocking idea that this innocent man would die for you, knowing everything about you—*everything*—and would step in between your own sin and a loving, perfect God.

Last but not least, we can acknowledge that everything is not all right in our world—or in our own lives. One of the most common misconceptions I've seen, within and without religious communities, is that we think we are good. We think that a person, left to his or her own devices, will do the right thing more often than not. I've seen too much of the world to believe that this is true. I believe everyone has a sense of right or wrong, in that we know how we want to be treated. But I know myself, and I want what I want. Most of us would choose the most selfish path possible to get what we want. When we admit to others that we struggle to do what is right, that we often make mistakes, we're setting the stage for honest dialogue about our need to be saved; about our need for a Savior.

"Never fail to speak up on a matter of the greatest consequence."

JOHN PEPPER, AMERICAN BUSINESS EXECUTIVE

Leading with our own humanity. Leading with compassion. Leading with finding common ground and asking good questions. These are the ways to build a bridge to a lasting relationship that just might give us the right to talk about the things we feel are worth fighting for. But more important, if we lead with love, we never lose the bigger fight for eternity.

LOVE

This is what it's all about: love.

Not a warm, fuzzy feeling that's mostly hormonal and makes you feel like you're being injected with a liter of chocolate. But a love that makes people willing to lay down their lives for what they believe in, and not just because they think they're right.

So often, we rush to defend ourselves and our reputations. If someone says something about me behind my back, my first instinct is to get angry. This is because I think my reputation is my own. I think I have something to be offended over. But I am not my own. I do not own myself, and there are particular rights that I give up when I say that I believe in Jesus. Specifically, the so-called right to be personally offended.

We defend our ideas and personal tastes. We have favorite football teams, bands, actors, flavors, colors, and brands, and anyone who disagrees with us clearly has bad taste. At least, it's my tendency to think so.

It's great to have well-defined personal tastes, to know what we like. Hey, people like people who like things. I've seen the research. But preferences can get out of hand. We see massive soccer games turn into big fights where people are injured and killed because of loyalty to a sports team. On a smaller scale, we see people argue and get worked up over someone's dislike of their favorite movie.

This is a misappropriation of everything we have. Nothing is ours. None of these things are that precious.

Think back to your last argument and ask yourself, *Was it worth it?* Most disagreements are petty at best. We take offense because we are prideful. Sometimes our expectations are not met, and we get mad at people because we expected them to simply know what we wanted to be done. Arguments, unmet expectations, pride—these are all reasons why people break up, or stop being friends, or hold grudges.

We need to be the people, the chivalrous men and women, who don't stoop to that level. Or rather, the men and women who rise above the level that we are naturally inclined to and instead fight for what really matters.

THE PROBLEM OF VIOLENCE

Violence is defined as "physical force exerted for the purpose of violating, damaging, or abusing."[2] We see violence in the news, in our neighborhoods, in our homes. Sadly, there's war and carnage all over the place.

Young people think they have to prove themselves by tests of physical strength or by who can draw faster and shoot another human being. Gang wars.

Adults want what another person has—and steal to get it.

Countries want another country's wealth or resources, so they take by force at the expense of human lives.

Senseless, meaningless killings. Without rhyme or reason.

Perhaps most frightening, people kill because it makes sense to them. These sick people enjoy it.

The way of the world seems to be brute force. If diplomacy, protocol, and kindness "don't work," we resort to violence.

Even when we open up the Bible, we're confronted with violence—from the Old Testament wars to the New Testament crucifixion.

There are people who try to ignore this. There are people who paint Jesus as a meek and gentle lamb who wouldn't hurt a fly. Jesus *is* described as a lamb in the Bible. Most famously, perhaps, by John the Baptist, one of the manliest guys in biblical history. (This guy wore camel skins, grew out his beard and his hair, lived in the desert, and ate dead locusts dipped in honey. He was like a scary mix between a dirty Oregon hipster and survival expert Bear Grylls.) "John saw Jesus coming toward him and said, 'Look! The Lamb of God who takes away the sin of the world!'" (John 1:29). A lamb used to be a sacrifice for the Jewish people as atonement for things they had done wrong. John's words were indicating a switch. Jesus was to be the final Lamb that would be sacrificed.

While some see Jesus only as an obedient Lamb, there are others who take the opposite extreme, portraying Jesus as a tough-guy superhero. One popular pastor claimed that "real men" avoid church because they're turned off by its portrayal of Christ as wimpy and unmasculine. This pastor said in a sermon, "Jesus was not a long-haired . . . effeminate-looking dude. . . ." Jesus had "callused hands and big biceps. . . . [An] Ultimate Fighting Jesus."[3]

Let me step in and say that a passive Jesus is not my Jesus, and a senselessly violent, angry Jesus is not mine either. I don't think either description paints a true picture of the Jesus we read about in the Bible.

My friend Shane makes his own clothes and bread, drives next to never, and has really good dreadlocks for a white guy. He lives in a commune in inner-city Philadelphia. One of Shane's big points is that, in the face of injustice, violence and complete passivity are equally wrong.

At an event where we were both speaking, I heard him say, "There is nothing worth killing for, but there are so many things worth dying for."

I want so badly for this to be true. There's the old adage "You have to fight fire with fire." We see this every day, in logical arguments that escalate and become shouting matches. When two people match each other's intensity, it doesn't make anyone feel better or make two people like each other more.

In light of much of the violence in the world today, including a massive shooting in a movie theater about forty-five minutes from where I wrote this chapter, controversial issues have once again been thrust to the front of everyone's minds. There are different views on gun control. There are different views on how the military should operate, especially in light of US armed forces in the Middle East. Questions come up, such as whether or not it is okay to hit your enemies before they hit you (also known as a preemptive strike). I have my own opinions, some of which are still forming and all of which I hold with an open hand. But I'm pretty sure that it's not as simple as some convinced people make it sound. The stuff these people shout on TV and on the Internet all sounds too easy.

"Take away their guns!"

"Give them all guns. It's in the Constitution!"

"Violence is never the answer!"

"We have to defend our way of life!"

Instead of choosing either violence or complete complacency, I have heard of an elusive third way of dealing with issues. I don't know what this would be called. Diplomacy? Telling someone about Jesus while they're pointing a gun at you? I'm not sure.

However, I am of the opinion that violence should never be the first thing we choose. It should be used only after all nonviolent options have been considered and found ineffective. Honestly, I think there are times when violence is understandable and maybe even appropriate. For example, if you have to defend yourself or someone else against a sudden violent attack, it makes sense to use force. But even in these cases, violence shouldn't be celebrated as fun or cool. There are consequences to using force to solve problems, and we shouldn't minimize the price we pay when we choose violence. Violence is not strength. I saw an online comment on this, saying, *"We need to stop maligning the choice to resolve conflict with words, instead of violence, as weakness."*[4]

For us chivalrous people, those of us following the Prince of Peace, who is also the Lion of Judah, the way of the world must be confronted with what is true. So what does the Bible say about violence?

First, we see that what we do in our minds is extremely important.

This is the message you heard from the beginning:
We should love one another. Do not be like Cain,
who belonged to the evil one and murdered his brother.
And why did he murder him? Because his own actions
were evil and his brother's were righteous. Do not be
surprised, my brothers and sisters, if the world hates
you. We know that we have passed from death to life,

because we love each other. Anyone who does not love
remains in death. Anyone who hates a brother or sister
is a murderer, and you know that no murderer has
eternal life residing in him.

1 JOHN 3:11-15, NIV

In Matthew 5, we see this same parallel between what happens in our minds and hearts compared to a seemingly more severe action in real life: If we want to have sex with people other than our spouses, we are adulterers in our hearts.[5] If we hate someone, we are murderers at heart.[6]

We are called to a higher standard, in our actions and in our thoughts. The 1 John 3 passage above says that we should love each other and that we should not be surprised when we are hated. Hatred is the way of those not set apart, those not saved. We should expect hatred from others. But we cannot afford to hate them. It taints our goodness. It spoils our fruit.

If violence is ever acceptable, we have to recognize the difference between protecting or sticking up for someone or something, and exacting a personal vendetta. Reluctant violence versus eager revenge. Fighting others because you don't like them or they don't like you is never acceptable. We will dislike people—sometimes for how they treat us, sometimes because they just annoy us.

We must also combat anything rooted in pride. Anything that is for self-glorification or is based in selfish ambition. We might feel like the author of this psalm:

Surely God is good to Israel,
to those who are pure in heart.

> But as for me, my feet had almost slipped;
> I had nearly lost my foothold.
> For I envied the arrogant
> when I saw the prosperity of the wicked. . . .
> They are free from common human burdens;
> they are not plagued by human ills.
> Therefore pride is their necklace;
> they clothe themselves with violence.
>
> PSALM 73:1-3, 5-6, NIV

It seems as if some people get away with murder. But are we cloaked in violence and pride? If this is what people who oppose us and who oppose God are dressed in, suited up with violence and pride, what should we strive to cover ourselves with?

PREPARING FOR BATTLE

There's an image in the Bible about what we should wear spiritually, what we should put on. The metaphor of combat is used here. We are told, "Put on the full armor of God so that you can take your stand against the devil's schemes. For our struggle is not against flesh and blood, but against the rulers, against the authorities, against the powers of this dark world and against the spiritual forces of evil in the heavenly realms."[7]

As a kid growing up in a Christian home, going to Christian schools and churches my whole life, I felt like people beat the "armor of God" concept to death. They would bring out a guy dressed in plasticky armor, with little cards taped to it: "breastplate of righteousness," "helmet of salvation," and the rest. I guess we were supposed to think it was cool, but I just got so tired of it that it lost its meaning to me. Now, though, I realize that this word picture, this metaphor of armor, really lends itself to the whole idea of chivalry, of us as knights in armor preparing for battle.

Let the truth be like a belt around your waist. Surrounding you. Holding your pants up.

Your chest is protected with righteousness, not because you are godly but because you have God inhabiting your soul, allowing his righteousness to be in you.

Your feet should be ready. Ready to tell the gospel, the good news of *peace*. Wear this like sandals. Laced up and ready to go.

Your shield, your defense, is not how much you know or how confident you are. What do you carry in front of yourself to deflect the flaming arrows shot at you? Faith. Your own goodness or "following your heart" or "believing in yourself" won't keep a flaming arrow (shot by the devil himself) from plunging in between your ribs. Faith is a shield made of "being sure of what we hope for and certain of what we do not see."[8]

For further protection, your salvation will be your helmet. The covering for your head is that you have been saved from the punishment of sin. Accept God's salvation, and your head is covered.

Finally, take up your one offensive weapon. This is what you will use in combat to strike back. Not your own fists or your smarts or your physical strength. Not your cynicism or who your parents are or how much money you have or your excuses for why you can't do anything. Your sword is the sword of the Spirit, the Word of God, known for being "living, and active, and sharper than any two-edged sword, and piercing even to the dividing of soul and spirit, of both joints and marrow, and quick to discern the thoughts and intents of the heart."[9]

It's so sharp that it separates the soul from the spirit. The soul may be described as our mind, maybe even our flesh. Our soul is concerned with the temporary things we think of and desire. Our physical being. Our needs. Our welfare. The spirit is the metaphysical power by which we prefer the things of God, the timeless things, to those that are immediate and fleeting. This is how we pursue what is good, true, and beautiful above all else. This allows us to look in a mirror at what we long for, at our thought life, at what we hold in our little mind jars, and to compare it with what is actually best.

We may think there are humans who are our enemies. People who are "wicked," who seem to only want to do harm to us and to others. But if their armor is made of pride and violence, they are not as strong as they appear. We know that pride comes before destruction, and he who lives violently will die violently.[10]

We need to realize that we aren't really fighting each other. We aren't fighting people. We are battling principles. This is why it is important to fight for what matters.

Make no mistake: *Peace is not a tolerance of evil.*

Doing nothing while evil is happening is as bad as being an attacker. Standing by complacently makes us accomplices.

So what do we do? We resolve to . . .

Never. Fight. Needlessly.

Neither physically nor verbally.

But we also have a responsibility to not look the other way when people are abusing their power.

It has been said, "All that is necessary for the triumph of evil is that good [people] do nothing."[11] We must seek God for wisdom to know when to stand, when to turn away, when to defend.

JUSTICE AND DAILY LIFE

My generation has exhibited a lot of passion for issues of social justice. That is to say, my generation has at the very least expressed interest in helping people and in making that pursuit a part of our lives.

When I speak, I often encourage audiences not to let their compassion extend only to people who live close to them or look like them. I tell people (with a pretty cheesy, churchy illustration) that God didn't look down on us and say we were different, that we were too far away to save. He came to us.

I still believe that, but I've witnessed the opposite end of that spectrum. It's another extreme within the church: often we care more about people halfway around the world than we do about people in our own homes, workplaces, schools, and houses of worship.

The prophet Isaiah said, "Seek justice. Help the oppressed. Defend the cause of orphans. Fight for the rights of widows."[12]

Do we think this applies only to one set of people? Can we buy TOMS shoes and sponsor a kid through Compassion International, and then treat our families like trash? Do we think that we can vote to be a voice for the voiceless, and then look the other way when someone is mistreated in our community? Do we think we can sign petitions and click "like" when it comes to fighting injustice around the world, and then ignore racial slurs, bigoted remarks, and insults thrown at others?

The answer has to be, *No!*

I hope that we have already established that our words and actions both matter.

While researching for my second book, *Generation Change*, I came across an article called "The Day Racism Hit Home" by Dara Fisk-Ekanger. This article appeared in an online magazine called *Boundless*, and I included a chunk of it in the chapter about unity. Dara wrote about a young Latino man who became close friends with a white girl. The guy was well respected in the community and in their school, but the girl's father was enraged over their friendship—simply because the young man had skin that was a darker shade of brown than that of his daughter. Dara talks about how the Bible challenges racial bigotry:

> "There is neither Jew nor Greek . . . for you are all one" (Galatians 3:28). "I looked and saw . . . [members] from every nation, tribe, people and language, standing before the throne [of God]" (Revelation 7:9).
>
> Forget the "separate but equal" stuff. God intends us to learn from one another, to let the best qualities of peoples and cultures rub off on each other. . . . The Lausanne Covenant eloquently puts it, "Because man is God's creature, some of his culture is rich in beauty and goodness. Because he is fallen, all of it is tainted with sin."[13]

She continues by describing how we all descended from the same people. We are all *one* people. We are united in our humanity regardless of skin tone or ethnic heritage. I believe that, through relationships and truly getting to know people different from us, racism has little chance. My life has been enriched by having deep and meaningful relationships with people who don't share my skin tone. By listening to the hurts caused throughout history and by seeking to understand the depth of others' pain, we can be part of the solution. As Dara says, "We can stand up for those who are suffering under the unjust prejudices of blind and deceived individuals. But we must guard our own actions and thoughts, lest we become as hate-filled as those we oppose."[14]

FIGHTING FOR EQUALITY

There is a particular kind of division that is especially harmful and shouldn't exist in God's family. It's been said for a while that the church is the most segregated place in America.

In my own experience, this appears to be true—and to me it's very sad. As I've studied the abolition of slavery and looked at other human rights issues, I have felt ashamed by what people have done to each other.

As chivalrous people, we need to make the first move to nurture transracial friendships, especially in church. But we must recognize that it may take some time to earn trust and respect. We can't expect to overcome racial and cultural boundaries immediately just because our intentions are good, or because we were not directly involved in the horrors of something like slavery.

I can be really close to people of other races, but I'll never know completely what it's like to *be* them.

There's often a lack of trust that stems from a whole history of past offenses that each person carries into relationships. So whatever your racial background, if you try to reach out and there are no immediate breakthroughs—if you're being kept at arm's length—you have to decide whether you're going to be patient and continue to show love, acceptance, and a desire for true friendship, or whether you're going to cut and run.

Selfishness and pride are the root causes of many divisions

among people. Remember, unity isn't just racial—it's relational. To break down boundaries, we must build understanding and find common ground. Instead of pointing out where we think someone else is wrong, we should find and build on something we agree upon. We don't always have to prove how much we know; sometimes it's better to just listen.

My dad often talks about "the power of the question." He says when you're seeking to understand someone else or facing a tense or difficult situation, asking questions and really listening can be a great way to move forward. "So, what was it like growing up in your town/city/neighborhood?" "What kinds of concerns or fears did you have as a kid?" "What did you think or hope you would be when you grew up?" Then he suggests that you be ready to answer the same questions yourself if you are asked.

So how do racism and cross-cultural relationships fit into a chapter titled "I Will Fight Only for the Sake of Those Who Are Unable to Defend Themselves, or in the Defense of Justice"? I hope it's obvious that I think it's a good thing to stand up for others who are the recipients of any kind of pain or injustice. But what does it mean to fight for them?

We stand up when someone is being marginalized. When someone is being mocked or when we see something that would hurt the progress of unity, we speak out. To follow the way of chivalry, we cannot afford to be silent.

VI

I Will Honor Truth and Always Keep My Promises.

"To rise from error to truth is rare and beautiful."

VICTOR HUGO

TRUTHFUL = TRUSTWORTHY

We often tell someone, "Yeah, let's hang out" or "I'll pray for you." And then we never do what we say we'll do, or we never get back in touch with the person. Honorable ladies and gentlemen give their word only when they can deliver on their promises. And once a promise is made, it is kept. Part of being just is also being truthful.

Our flippant and even untruthful comments can also damage relationships. These days our communication is magnified by mobile devices and styles since we can tweet, text, or comment to one person or millions of people in milliseconds. What does our casual attitude about telling the truth say about our spiritual commitment? Truthful people are more trustworthy—promise keepers are dependable. Both are the kind of people we should be and should surround ourselves with.

MY PROM STORY

MY FAMILY MOVED FROM GEORGIA to Colorado during winter break of my senior year of high school. I wasn't too upset about moving away from Georgia, honestly. The church I went to was great, but I had only three or four friends total. So the move wasn't so bad for me.

On top of that, I had lived in the exact same town we were moving to when I was in elementary school, and I'd be returning to the same school I had gone to as a kid. I had also spoken at this school a couple of years before. This could have made things awkward, and sometimes it did. There was also the fact that I'm naturally an introvert. I really like people, but I can be pretty shy.

I already had more than enough credits to graduate, but I thought taking a few classes might help me get reacquainted with some old friends and maybe make a few new ones. So I decided to introduce myself to every single person in all of my classes. In hindsight, it probably seemed a little strange to my classmates.

There was one girl named Jennifer. She was very pretty— a ballerina and former cheerleader. I asked her to have coffee a couple of times. I'll admit that it was for a shallow reason. She was cute. But as I got to know her outside of school, I saw that she acted differently when it was just us drinking coffee. She seemed less intentional. At school, she flirted a lot, which isn't unusual in high school. But through hanging out with her away from school, I saw that she thought all of her worth was in her external appearance.

One time we were eating at this place called La Baguette, a really chill, very French café. I said to her, "You know, sometimes I meet people, and I feel like I can tell different things about them by how they remind me of other people."

"Oh?" she said. "Do I remind you of anybody?"

Pause for a second, guys. I was probably supposed to say, "No, you're one of a kind! I've never met anyone like you!"

Instead I said, "Actually, yeah!"

Then I proceeded to tell this story about another girl I knew— someone who was pretty and attracted a lot of attention. I said,

"I feel as though you act like her, like your looks are your worth. Like you think that's all you are."

She started crying, which was not something I had expected. It was awkward. But she thanked me for my honesty, and we hung out a few more times after that.

Toward the end of the year I thought, *Hey, she would be a cool person to take to prom.*

So I went out for coffee with Jennifer again and said, "Hey, I have a question for ya. Would you . . . do me the honor of going to prom with me?"

She looked shocked. Then, after a painfully long pause, she said, "Sorry, it was like someone dropped an ice cube down my shirt. Yes! Yes, I'd love to go with you!"

Fast-forward a couple of weeks. I was at an Owl City show with my dad. We were having a good night. But about three-quarters of the way through the set, I got this text: "Hey, Zach, I'm so sorry, but I can't go to prom with you. I already promised someone else I would go with them a year ago plus I made other plans with friends so . . . I'm sorry but I can't go to prom with you."

I was absolutely stunned at first. But then, I felt like I should have expected it. I've always had low self-esteem and thought I was ugly. This is not the kind of thing you probably expect to hear from a guy. But believe me, girls aren't the only ones who struggle with these feelings.

I called her the next day. She said that her friends were upset with her for having a date, because they had all agreed to go as a group without dates (which clearly didn't jibe with what she had texted me). I told her so. I said that her statements in the text obviously couldn't have been the truth, and if she just didn't want to go with me, she should have said so.

She said, "I thought we were just friends. And I thought you knew that. But clearly you thought there was more going on."

My response: "No. I thought we *were* friends. Friends don't lie to friends. Friends don't play with their friends' feelings. I thought we were friends. Clearly I was wrong."

Later I talked to a friend named Carl, a kid I had grown up with when we lived in Colorado before. I told him what Jennifer had said and how it couldn't be the truth.

He said, "That really stinks, man! Are you gonna find someone else to go with?"

"I don't really know," I said.

After a week or so of additional drama, I decided not to go to prom at all. Instead I went to the Biola Media Conference in Los Angeles where I got to meet Ralph Winter (the producer of the X-Men movies). While I was there, I checked Facebook to see who Carl went to prom with. I couldn't believe my eyes. *No . . . no way. Is that . . . ?*

There they were, Carl and Jennifer, both dressed in their prom best.

I definitely did not expect that.

I thought maybe Jennifer had asked him as a way to get out of going with me. Or maybe he had asked her in the in-between, and we just hadn't talked about it.

I found out later that he had asked her to prom after I talked with him. He asked her in the school hallway, with a bouquet of flowers, on bended knee. And she went with him.

The point of this story is not about how much my life stunk in high school. I had some good times. And I'm exceedingly grateful that I didn't stay stuck in relationships that wouldn't have ended well.

The point is that there are many types of honesty. This story could have gone in the chapter about not attacking from behind.

I'm not trying to defame anyone; that's why I used different names. But I tell this story to demonstrate that honesty is necessary to relationship. If we can learn from the little pains in each other's lives without having to go through the same thing, we will probably be much wiser for the shared wear. If we have a difficult situation and we want to or need to get out of it, we must do so honestly. If we don't, it might cost us friendships. It most certainly may hurt people we say we care about.

WHAT HONESTY ISN'T

"I will never lie. 'I will honor truth and always keep my promises.' What does this mean to you?" I asked my friend Jonas, the artist-anarchist.

He said, "Lying is common courtesy in this culture. You can be 100 percent honest if you like—but a lot of people will not like you. I think courtesy lies are fine, but there is a line separating those from 'fo' real' lies. I think everyone should keep their promises. Duh. Not many people do though. I try extra hard on this count, and even I've blown it a couple of times."

The term *courtesy lies* (or white lies) might be a bit edgy or sound a little dangerous to us. What if we think of it in terms of *gentle truth*? I'm not saying we should lie when we don't want to tell the truth. What I'm saying is, if someone asks, "Does this dress make me look fat?" you never respond, "Yes. Yes, it does. Soooo fat. Like, seriously. Fatfatfat." No, you offer a genuine but generic compliment, like, "Wow! You look great!"

Maybe this chapter should be titled "I Will *Do My Best* to Be Honest" (thanks to my Facebook friend Krista for pointing this out) because it's basically impossible to be 100 percent truthful 100 percent of the time. We may accidentally exaggerate or not give a completely direct answer. Sometimes we will omit details just for the sake of being polite and not being hurtful.

Think of questions like "Did you like your liver and onions?" when it was served for dinner at someone's house, or "What does he have that I don't have?" if your boyfriend asks what you think of some other guy.

I remember this plot in many popular, educational kids' TV shows. One of the characters gets in trouble for lying, and some-one tells him that he should tell the truth all the time. So the kid starts telling people that they're annoy-ing and fat and that their breath smells bad. Then some loving adult explains to him that you don't have to say something just because it's true; you don't always have to voice your opinion. Then everyone laughs, and it fades to black as the credits roll.

> *"A lie gets halfway around the world before the truth has a chance to get its pants on."*
> WINSTON CHURCHILL

TELLING THE TRUTH AND HEARING *THE TRUTH*

Speaking the gentle truth is also important for those people who claim to have a special gift that sounds extremely mystical and magical: the Gift of Perception. This seems to mean that they are able to understand things about you that are suppos-edly beneficial for you to know. Often they believe this ability has been imparted to them as a gift by the Holy Spirit. Let's look at the place in the Bible where this theory may come from:

> There are different kinds of spiritual gifts, but the same
> Spirit is the source of them all. There are different
> kinds of service, but we serve the same Lord. God

works in different ways, but it is the same God who does the work in all of us.

A spiritual gift is given to each of us so we can help each other. To one person the Spirit gives the ability to give wise advice; to another the same Spirit gives a message of special knowledge. The same Spirit gives great faith to another, and to someone else the one Spirit gives the gift of healing. He gives one person the power to perform miracles, and another the ability to prophesy. He gives someone else the ability to discern whether a message is from the Spirit of God or from another spirit. Still another person is given the ability to speak in unknown languages, while another is given the ability to interpret what is being said. It is the one and only Spirit who distributes all these gifts. He alone decides which gift each person should have.

I CORINTHIANS 12:4-11

I was reading a commentary (a book that helps you study the Bible) written by this guy, Matthew Henry. He explained how a lot of people in Corinth were claiming to have awesome spiritual powers, and Paul (the author of two letters to the people there) was basically cautioning the Corinthians not to be gullible. These gifts were supposed to help in spreading the Good News to people and to show that these followers of Jesus were different. Matthew Henry reiterates the fact that spiritual gifts are given to us for the purpose of helping others—not just building ourselves up.[1]

If this gift of perception is really from God, then it will be used for building people up—not putting them in their place.

Maybe you've had this experience: A Christian friend comes to you and says he has a "word from the Lord" for you. And then he tells you something about you or your life. That's not so bad, but maybe this friend frequently offers you thoughts on how you can improve yourself, or tries to psychoanalyze you so he can pass off his own opinions as spiritual wisdom. I'm not saying there's never any truth to these opinions—or even that they're often untrue. But if someone gives you advice or tells you what's wrong with you—and it doesn't cause you to grow in your faith—then it may not be from God. It may be a well-meaning friend's idea.

Be careful in the context of friendships with other Christians not to absorb all they feel you should do and be. Seek the truth. Love the truth. And rely on wise advice from your mentors who know you well—yet another reason we don't walk this journey alone.

If you find yourself often wanting to tell people what they should do—or how they should be—take care not to misuse your relationship with the person to whom you are talking. Be truthful. If it's your opinion, make sure you are clear on that. And if it's only your opinion, you may want to keep it to yourself. In the name of spiritual growth, we can sometimes do damage to people who are supposed to be like our brothers and sisters.

We must be extremely careful not to attribute things to God that we come up with ourselves. Some may not call that lying— but is it telling the truth?

BRUTALLY HONEST

I have this friend who prides herself on being blunt. Let's call her Amy. People have told her over and over that she's really perceptive, that when she speaks it seems like she's seeing straight into their lives. But sometimes Amy uses this as an excuse to criticize. She often tries to psychoanalyze me—like I'm her project more than her friend—and even draws conclusions that are not true because, in fact, she doesn't know me *that* well. It doesn't feel great. At times I feel like she takes advantage of the trust in her friendships to just blurt out what she thinks—regardless of how it will make others feel.

This is another sort-of-false honesty. Brutal honesty.

Don't be that guy—or girl. Don't be a brutally honest lady or gentleman. Brutality has little to do with chivalry. It's interesting to see that brutal honesty is acceptable in people we agree with. A comedian or political commentator who shares our point of view can be outrageous or rude toward the opposition, and we think he's funny and cool. But if we disagree with the same comedian or commentator, we think he's mean or judgmental. Brutal honesty can be a weapon.

I see more brutally honest people in academic circles and in Christian circles than I have seen anywhere else. I believe in absolute truth, but I'm okay with the fact that people practice their faith differently. Truth isn't only about being right. We can let different opinions about theology divide us—or we can choose to respect each other. People often disagree about how God's Spirit is expressed and displayed in our lives, for example, but that's not the truth that ultimately sets us free. We need to leave room for individual opinions on side issues, while holding fast to the core truth of Jesus' life, death, and resurrection.

The gospel is about how much God loves us, the fact that he gave his only Son for us. It sounds impossible. It sounds completely crazy and illogical. But I believe it. If you confess with your mouth and believe in your heart that Jesus is Lord, you are a step closer to transcending your flesh, your human nature.[2] You are saved from eternal suffering and separation from the one who made you. For me, everything comes back to this. Not personal preferences or political affiliations. Christianity is not based on how you interpret gray areas in the Bible or who you vote for. Christianity is believing that Jesus did what the Bible says he did, that he is who he says he is.

Stating your opinion loudly, name-calling, being honest to a fault, inflicting pain—this is not how a chivalrous truth teller behaves.

It may be easier for some of us to be brutally honest, but chivalry is not about what's easy. It's about what's right.

Sarcasm, bluntness, brutal honesty, and masking the truth in a layer of pride or humor are really nothing more than an abuse of the truth.

HOW TO BE HONEST—AND WHY IT IS IMPORTANT

We've been talking a lot about what not to do, who not to be like, and what not to say. But the most important part of Truth is not what it isn't but what it is.

Speak the Truth in love.

Honesty is important because it's one of the few ways people know they can trust us. Trustworthiness and integrity are two integral parts of being a chivalrous man or woman.

By making a habit of being graciously honest, by letting the truth be known in situations where things are being muddied by subjectivity, personal emotions, and conflicting viewpoints, we can be fresh voices. We can illuminate the truest truth for people—shine the light on it so people can find their way.

Gentle truth told by a good friend, even when it may have a little sting, can bring us closer to each other and closer to God. Also, how you receive truth from others tells a lot about how humble or proud you are.

I have a friend named Ryan. This guy fights in cages and has a radio show. His dad does a lot of traditional, family-oriented, nonprofit work. Ryan wrote this book called *Be Intolerant: Because Some Things Are Just Stupid*, which is pretty controversial in a world obsessed with tolerance. Some of his delivery (let alone the title) may be a little abrasive, but one big thing that stood out to me was how hard-line he was on "speaking the truth in love." I like that. There's that old adage, "If you don't have anything nice to say, don't say anything at all." Sometimes I have shied away from saying something helpful because I thought it wasn't nice or clean; because confrontation was uncomfortable and I have worried about how people might view me afterward. There are times when confrontation is necessary, but it can still be done in love.

For example, imagine you have two friends who get in a serious argument. Afterward, one of them holds a grudge against the other. You can go to that person privately and say, "I think you're holding on to this way too tightly. Your friendship is more important than this grudge. At the very least, you need to let go of this anger for yourself and forgive your friend."

Some of you may have heard this really quotable passage of Jesus' teachings about not judging people:

> Do not judge, or you too will be judged. For in the
> same way you judge others, you will be judged, and
> with the measure you use, it will be measured to you.

Why do you look at the speck of sawdust in your brother's eye and pay no attention to the plank in your own eye? How can you say to your brother, "Let me take the speck out of your eye," when all the time there is a plank in your own eye? You hypocrite, first take the plank out of your own eye, and then you will see clearly to remove the speck from your brother's eye.

MATTHEW 7:1-5, NIV

This perspective will help us be humble in our approach if we have to confront people about their behavior, if we absolutely have to tell them the truth about how hurtful they have been. We need to be realistic about our own issues—realizing we have a log in our own eye. Again, the truth can become blurred or distorted if we are trying to shine it through the filter of our own point of view and if we don't fully acknowledge that we are as bad as everyone else. We have to be careful how and when we tell the truth.

LURED TO LIE

Everyone has lied or at least exaggerated at some point. I wondered *why*.

I asked my friends on the Internet (because the Internet is full of very opinionated people) the following question: "Why do people lie?" Here's what I got:

- "Fear and insecurities"
- "Fear of judgment" or "Not wanting to be judged or looked upon in a certain way"
- "Thinking so highly of yourself that you want to be accepted in people's eyes no matter the cost"

All good answers. When it comes down to it, most lies are motivated by fear, insecurity, or shame. Do any of these sound familiar?

You keep something from someone else because you are afraid of being found out. Maybe you go somewhere you aren't supposed to go. Maybe you're hanging out with a girl who's not your girlfriend (when you are, in fact, in a relationship with another girl).

Maybe you forget that an assignment is due. Suddenly "The dog ate it" or "My computer crashed" sounds appealing.

Or maybe a friend tells you a secret that could put your friend or somebody else in danger if you keep it. Something liked a planned crime, an eating disorder, abuse, or a suicide attempt. You may be afraid to tell anyone, because you feel like you would be betraying your friend. But you can't be afraid to tell the truth—*especially* in a situation where someone may be in danger.

Of course, there also are going to be times when it is to your benefit to lie.

To be untruthful.

To stretch the truth.

To hide the facts.

To dodge a question.

To stretch your accomplishments a bit.

But these, too, come out of insecurity. I have heard others talk about whom they know, or what somebody said to them, or things they've done. They put an emphasis on all of the good things. I know I've told stories to make myself sound good in an effort to belong; not stories that were blatantly dishonest but stories that cast me in a better light. Stories that put an emphasis on someone finding me attractive. Or stories that played up a specific instance to make me seem good at sports or another activity.

We all want to belong. We want to feel included and cared about and protected, and that is why fear and insecurity are two things we have to guard against in trying to be truth tellers.

It's easy to exaggerate. We want to be looked upon as fascinating or attractive. But we must be careful not to allow ourselves to be lured into lying. We cannot allow it to become an easy habit in our lives. We must commit to being truth tellers, people who are fully trustworthy, so others can always take us at our word.

I've betrayed people's trust before by doing something they *specifically* asked me not to do. Or by sharing a secret that wasn't mine to share—it was mine to keep. But if we are the kind of people who make a habit of being graciously honest, people can trust us. If we tell people when something is wrong or when they hurt our feelings, if we are honest in tough situations without being mean, people can trust us. And if we don't try to exaggerate or fib to cover our backs or puff ourselves up, people will know we are genuine. Trust can be fleeting; integrity and honesty are enduring.

Make it your goal to never lie and to always keep your promises. A chivalrous person honors truth.

VII

I WILL FEAR NO EVIL.

"I learned that courage was not the absence of fear, but the triumph over it. The brave man is not he who does not feel afraid, but he who conquers that fear."

NELSON MANDELA

WHY WE ARE AFRAID OF THE DARK

I don't remember being afraid of much when I was a little kid. Which is funny, because I had a clinical anxiety disorder for years. Not really hilarious, but still ironic.

I do remember one time, specifically, when I was scared out of my mind. I screamed and probably cried and almost wet my pants. It was bad.

It happened in our little yellow house in Colorado Springs, the house where most of my earliest memories come from. I remember stepping on a LEGO brick as the most painful thing ever. I remember not being allowed to play with Pokémon cards. I remember lots of moments spent with my parents, including playing hide-and-seek with my dad one night.

I was young, maybe five or six. My head barely came up to most of the doorknobs. I looked for my dad all over downstairs, but I couldn't find him. So I went upstairs. There was my parents' bedroom on the left, mine on the right. Then down the hall I could see the doors to the office and the guest room. The office door was open, and the light was off. I felt like Sherlock Holmes. I was sure the door hadn't been open earlier, but now it was, slightly. He must be hiding in the office.

Elementary.

I crept up to the open door. . . .

"Daaaaad . . . Daaaaad . . . DaaaaAAAAHHHH!!!"

On the last *Dad* I heard the most terrifying sound I had ever experienced in my short life. It was the kind of sound that E.T.'s evil twin would make. And I've never liked E.T.

Have you ever heard someone whistle and hum at the same time, and it makes a *Twilight Zone*–spaceship sound? Well, I never had.

I screamed and ran down the stairs, sure I was about to die, yelling for my parents. My dad came out, trying not to laugh, and wrapped me up in his arms.

"It's okay, it's okay. It was me."

"What was that noise?"

Then I got a lesson on whistle humming. And that was that.

What's funny is that I wouldn't have been afraid of the sound if the light had been on.

This isn't abnormal for kids, I realize. The interesting part is that we don't have to be taught to be afraid of the dark. We're just scared of it. Not only for the sake of darkness but also because of what we can't see. Which could be . . . anything. We can't see anything if it's dark enough. That's why kids are afraid of the dark. Mostly because of the unknown, because they can't see what may or may not be there. But there's also a fear that evil lurks in the unknown.

We have this concept that *good* is what we know. That it can be easily seen. That if we don't know something, or if it isn't familiar, it's probably not good or useful. That evil hides out, lying in wait for us. In reality, sometimes it's the other way around. Maybe evil is right in front of us, in plain sight, and good is lying in wait for us. We often fear the shadows and think they're evil. Even shadows of doubt within our own minds.

Behind our fears, the major problem is that we humans

assume we're good. That whatever we have figured out on our own is the truth, and anything we don't understand is wrong.

I talked to a friend about this. Her name is Cozette. Anyone who knows Cozette could tell you that she really loves Jesus. She loves Jesus as if he is a real person who talks to her and loves her back. Which, I believe, he is. A lot of other people say they believe this, too, but few stand up on their tiptoes and bubble over with excitement when talking about someone whose teachings they follow. Cozette does.

I talked to Cozette about this whole concept of fear and evil. I thought someone like her might have some special knowledge the rest of us don't have.

Cozette had some interesting insights. She started off by saying, "Maybe this is coming out of left field. But when I think of fear, I think of being fearful of making decisions—of lacking the ability to make the right decision, more specifically. Or choosing something, and then being scared and doubtful after making my choice.

"One of my mentors was talking to me about this. He used this comparison: tightrope vs. playground. He said to me, 'You've approached life and God like walking a tightrope: afraid of falling off one side or the other. There's no forward motion; you're just standing there. You almost view the will of God as if you didn't have the ability to choose. You're driven by fear to not make choices. But when I take my kids to the playground, I could tell them to go up the stairs (walking not running), take three steps to the slide, go down cautiously, then climb once across the monkey bars, swing for exactly three minutes, and come back to me. But what gives me joy is to let my kids go and play freely, to know that the presence of their father is enough to guide them. I'm there. They know they're safe.'"

Instead of enjoying life's playground, we treat every day like a tightrope walk. We're obsessed with safety and familiarity. Cozette calls this the Tyranny of the Familiar, which we are prone to as humans. Comfort is the tyrant who dictates that fear is a good thing, that fear is our friend. We fear the unknown even if it's in our best interest. Our nature is to be fearful, but we must overcome our nature.

But I'm getting ahead of myself and starting to feel a little preachy. I don't like being preached at. But I do love stories.

THE PEOPLE IN THE CAVERN

ASHER BOLTED STRAIGHT UP IN HIS BED, gasping for air. There it was again. The dream. Families huddled inside a dark cave. The look of terror on their faces was so visceral, so hopeless. As if they had seen darkness itself. Evil itself.

As a child, Asher had heard stories about a great evil that lurked in the darkness. More vicious than the wolves of the mountain forests, its eyes glowing with evil like twin, sickly yellow moons. It had the body of a lion—but two times the size—and the tail of a scorpion, dripping with deadly poison. Worst of all, it had the face of a man with three rows of shark-like teeth, each the size of a human fist. It was said that when the beast talked, the sound was like three voices, all in a dissonant unison. It was the manticore.

Asher had never known his grandfather. The monster had taken him when Asher's father was just a boy. And now Asher, a young man of fifteen, experienced a similar loss. But it wasn't his father who had disappeared. It was Tamarah, the prettiest girl in the village. Asher had often been distracted by her beauty. Whenever Tamarah walked past the shop where he apprenticed, Asher was scolded for losing track of his work.

Now she was gone. Asher had felt his knees tremble when he heard, "Tamarah was taken."

Shortly before, whole families had disappeared in the night from the next village over. No bodies were ever found. The more frightened people became, the more the attacks increased. Asher remembered talking to Tamarah about the disappearances. She had been so afraid. Every night, she heard sounds outside. Muttering, like three voices all saying the same thing.

Asher told her she must have been dreaming. There must be a logical explanation. But she refused to hear. That very night she vanished—one week ago. They said there had been scratches on her bedposts. They said a fingernail was lodged in the wooden windowsill. They said there was blood.

Asher had awakened in the middle of every night since. Each time he reviewed the faces in his dream—and recognized them. Their pupils were dilated like those of animals, their mouths wide open with speechless terror.

Asher had not been afraid of the manticore before Tamarah's disappearance. But now, it was more than a story. Now, for the first time, he felt fear climbing up his chest and into his throat, searching for an opening. Then he heard it.

A murmuring, a muttering, a growling. *Only the wind*, he tried to reason. But the sound grew louder. He rose and crept to the window, pressing his back against the wall. He craned his neck, trying to hear what the voice was saying. In the night air, he smelled the strong aroma of sulfur.

No. NO! It can't be!

Asher was afraid.

It had come for him. In Asher's moment of fear, the manticore had come for him. There it stood, eclipsing the moon—the manticore. It stared at him with ghastly yellow eyes.

Asher's mind seemed to split in two: half flying at the speed of sound, with all his life's images and people and memories and hopes all converged into one; the other half holding steady, refusing to be overcome. He took a quick, deep breath and chose the calmer track.

What Asher did next surprised even him. He felt a swelling in his chest—not of terror, but of something warm that broke his temporary paralysis. He rose to his feet, his eyes locked on the demon. He spoke slowly, firmly. "I am afraid, but I will not die in fear. On my life, I dare you to take me, devil."

The manticore shrieked in three different unearthly voices and spun away. Asher saw the beast run away in the direction of the forest.

It had been frightened—the manticore had been frightened! He had resisted the devil, and it had fled.

Asher then remembered his grandfather's leather armor. From a trunk beneath his cot, he lifted the breastplate, put it on, and laced it up. He pulled the leather gauntlets onto his hands and lifted a blade from the bottom of the trunk. It was only a dagger, about six inches long. He grimaced. *I am to kill a devil with a kitchen knife?* he thought as he tucked the dagger under his belt. Quickly he tore off part of his tunic sleeve with his teeth, lashed it to the top of his walking stick, and soaked the rag with oil. Lighting the makeshift torch, he vaulted through the open window and charged after the manticore. The war cry from his lips ripped the silence of the night, surprising even him.

Asher crashed through the forest, scraping exposed skin on thorns and branches. But he did not fall. He felt his passion guiding him, keeping him upright as he pressed on. He had a plan: find the creature and stab it in the throat.

The manticore had left a trail of carnage, and Asher followed it to a cave. There beside the opening stood the demon. Speaking in one deep voice, the manticore said, "Boy! What possessed you to follow me?"

Asher stood there as if mute.

"*Speak*, manspawn! What do they call you?"

"Ash . . . Asher," he said. He cleared his throat and shouted, "They call me Asher! You took my grandfather many years ago, and now you have taken a friend." He looked straight into the yellow eyes of the beast. "I am here to kill you."

At this, the manticore unleashed a screaming roar that turned into a cackling laugh. Then, in an old woman's voice, the manticore said sweetly, "My dear, even if you were the strongest man on earth, you could not strike with enough force to harm me."

"What . . . I mean who . . . what is your name, demon?"

"My name is Geryon."

"Geryon, what have you done with Tamarah?"

"That lovely young maiden? Oh, I've put her in a safe place."

"Hellspawn! You have eaten her!"

"No, worm. I hurt no one. She is safe inside this cave."

"Are you not the manticore of legend? The child stealer, the widow maker?"

"I have heard they speak of me in such terms. I only take the fearful in the darkness and leave them here. They do the rest."

Asher's courage built slowly, as he saw the creature posed him no immediate threat. But his confusion built as well. "Do you mean that you do not kill people?"

The manticore laughed. "I have killed no sons or daughters of men."

"Then why do people fear you?"

"Because I am what all humans fear. I dwell in the unknown.

I lurk in the darkness. I am known but not understood. I am perceived as evil for, truly, that is what I am."

"But why do you take them?"

"I only take people who allow themselves to be taken. Those who have chosen to live in fear. They imprison themselves. They *choose* their fate. I just . . . assist them."

"So Tamarah and the others . . . they can leave the cave any time they want?"

"Yes, but no one has ever left. The cave is utterly dark. When they enter, fear dampens their senses. They gasp like fish with no water. They are many, but they are paralyzed by fear."

"What if someone took the light to them?"

"Oh, child." The manticore spoke in the old lady's voice again. "You do not fear, but you still lack understanding. The darkness is not evil. What is evil is their fear. Bound by ignorance, they will fear what they do not understand. Although they hate evil, they do nothing to combat it. And it consumes them."

Asher's courage continued to build. "I will go to her—to them!" he yelled, taking one slow step forward.

"Do what you like. You do not fear me, so I can do nothing!"

With that, Asher strode powerfully past Geryon, keeping his eyes locked on the beast's, and entered the dark mouth of the cave.

OUR THREE BIGGEST FEARS

Let's back up for a moment and talk about three things that people fear. Here, I wrote them down for you:

1. The unknown
2. What we know but do not understand
3. What we understand to be evil

In the Bible I see that perfect love is supposed to remove fear. It says, "There is no fear in love. But perfect love drives out fear, because fear has to do with punishment. The one who fears is not made perfect in love."[1]

Perfect. Love.

A few sentences earlier, the writer, John, tells us that if we do not love, we do not know God, because *God is love.*

John says, "We know and rely on the love God has for us. God is love. Whoever lives in love lives in God, and God in them."[2]

Fear of the unknown

Why do we fear the unknown? What is it about human nature that squeezes us into a state of discomfort when we are unfamiliar with something?

Fear of the unknown can mean many things to many people, but it also reminds me of racism. There's a big word for people who think in terms of *us* and *them*: xenophobia. My friend Dr. Merriam-Webster tells me that this means a "fear and hatred of strangers or foreigners or of anything that is strange or foreign."[3] The object of fear or hate is known, but whatever it is that makes this thing or person "different" is unknown. And that unknown is what justifies a racist's hate.

Xenophobia is more than just racism. It's more than a hatred of people who look different from us—it's a fear. In my opinion, most hatred that isn't right or good comes from fear. There are some things we should hate, like injustice and suffering. But we also hate a lot of things we shouldn't. We do not like to be afraid, yet we fear things. When it comes to facing the unknown, if we have no faith and we do not trust, we can easily hate and fear what we don't know.

This includes the dark, anything we can't see, even something as seemingly benign as moving to a new place. While a move can be filled with opportunity, it can also create pockets of fear and anxiety. I know a lot of people who have lived somewhat charmed lives in that they've moved maybe once throughout their entire existence. They've had the ability to retain the same community of friends. I've moved frequently in my life. I was born in Seattle, and I've lived in Virginia, Georgia, and Colorado. I've gone to many different schools and churches in my life too. But I was never a member of the in-group. That's not a slang term for "cool kids." It's the opposite of an out-group, those who are disliked or ostracized simply for being different. I just never really fit in anywhere specific in high school.

As a kid, I was afraid of rejection fairly consistently. Not so much anymore, honestly. But I still don't like going into a new place alone. Maybe that comes from years of conditioning when I learned that entering a new place or being the new person is something unpleasant and something to be feared. Maybe you can relate. But as I've gotten older and have been thrust into situations that would induce anxiety in most people, it's gotten easier to face the unknown.

I've heard that one way to overcome this type of fear is to prepare for the worst. I watched this video from a guy who had a vague fear of being stuck outdoors. He was a Boy Scout growing up, so it couldn't have been that terrible. But he had a test coming up where he would have to build a shelter and camp out overnight without his scoutmaster. He talked about being afraid of bears coming and eating him in his sleep. He said that as the event approached, the fear seemed to get bigger and bigger in his mind, and he didn't know what to do about it. Then it hit him. He should plan for the worst. He gathered as many supplies as he could and read every survival book he could get his hands on. In his mind, by prepping for the worst-case scenario, he would be ready for anything that could possibly go wrong.

I had a similar situation when I was growing up. For a while, I saw a therapist named Sharon Hersh, a friend of our family. I had a clinical anxiety disorder for the longest time. I Googled "clinical anxiety disorder" so I could sound more intelligent describing it to you, my dear reader. The Wikipedia article that came up first had a picture of the painting *The Scream* by Edvard Munch. I'm not sure if that is insensitive or ridiculously humorous. I think it is mostly funny.

Anyway, according to Wikipedia (the fount of knowledge that it is), "Anxiety disorder is a blanket term covering several different forms of a type of common psychiatric disorder characterized by excessive rumination, worrying, uneasiness, apprehension, and fear about future uncertainties either based on real or imagined events, which may affect both physical and psychological health. . . . The emotions present in anxiety disorders range from simple nervousness to bouts of terror."[4]

When I was younger, I had an irrational, yet extremely strong fear of becoming sick and throwing up. I had gotten really sick once with a virus that was like the stomach flu. For about ten days there was a lot of throwing up and feeling awful. I felt really out of control.

After that, I was afraid that I would get sick at school. That if I ate certain foods, I would throw up. I would get anxious before bed because I didn't want to have to wake up in the middle of the night throwing up.

I specifically remember a few times when I got so worked up over being scared to eat or go to school, that I curled up in a ball, inconsolable. I wouldn't listen to reason.

My parents tried to help me. I felt sick to my stomach all the time. I worked myself into having actual stomach problems. I was chomping chalky pills all day long.

Then I went to see Sharon. It made me nervous to even talk about getting sick.

But Sharon talked me through my fear. It seems really silly, retrospectively. She had me say, "Vomit, puke, barf, throw up, hurl, and toss your cookies." Over and over. This sounds crazy, right? I kid you not, I was nervous to even say those words.

Sharon asked me, "What are you afraid of?"

"I'm scared of . . . getting sick?"

"What's the worst that could happen if you got sick?"

"I could throw up!"

"What's the worst thing that could happen if you throw up?"

"I could *die*!"

"And then what happens when you die?"

"I . . . I go to heaven."

"Do you really believe that?"

I did.

Sharon asked me to face the worst and to accept it. This was freeing from fear, as opposed to playing into the fear by planning for the worst. If you prepare for the worst-case scenario, when are you done? Never. You can never plan enough. But when you face the worst and just accept it, you're free. Fear no longer has power over you.

Fear of what we don't understand

The next level of our human fear—things we are born fearing and that we are taught by our parents and teachers and culture to fear—is fear of things that we can see and recognize but that we do not understand. We tend to fear stuff that we don't "get."

If you've ever been called weird, you understand this. If you're one of those people who thinks everyone else is weird, you probably don't get this at all. This is why there are outcasts.

We can't be afraid of the way somebody chooses to do something differently. We can't think that our way is the right way all the time. I'm extremely guilty of this. I have a lot of opinions. About politics, theology, art—everything. I'm still struggling with a lot of music-related snobbery. (But seriously, in fifty years no one will remember Carly Rae Jepsen. If you're reading this fifty years—or maybe five months—into the future, please tell me I'm right.)

It gets much more serious than this, and I don't want to detract from the gravity of these situations.

Little boys who act slightly effeminate (or in what our culture decides is a feminine manner) are often ridiculed and sometimes beaten up.

We, as Christians, cannot tolerate this, let alone participate in it.

Girls who may not fit the Christian and Western cultural mold of the "gentle and quiet spirit" are thought to be rebellious or aggressive and are often put in their place.

We, as Christians, must not do this.

People who drive a car missing a few hubcaps, or who use food stamps at the market, or who wear stained shirts or too-short pants are sometimes viewed as inferior. Not just less financially fortunate, but inferior—not as valuable or important as other human beings.

We, as Christians, must not view them that way.

There are so many examples: Families with a different accent who may be difficult to understand—and difficult to convince your parents to let you ride with, because their "differentness" or "foreignness" makes them a risk. Someone who may dress differently or cover her hair with an unfamiliar scarf. Men who wear a hat, a beard, and long ringlets of hair. Aren't these strangers to be feared or at least suspected? I have heard someone's ethnic heritage spoken in the tone of a swear word, as though we believe nationality determines whether someone is evil and risky or good and safe.

We, as Christians, must refuse to believe this.

We the chivalrous must distinguish between the unknown, the unfamiliar, and the evil.

Fear of evil

I think we misunderstand what evil really is. We have already discussed how the unfamiliar or unknown are not necessarily evil. But we are eager to call things evil if we don't understand them. Some Christians condemn yoga as "demonic" because of its origins in Eastern mysticism. But these same people might practice martial arts, which are rooted in the same type of mysticism.

In the context of the scriptural assurance that we can overcome evil with good,[5] we need to draw a few distinctions:

- We need to be able to hate evil without living in fear of it.
- We need to love people who are different from us—yes, even people we think are wrong—and not label them as evil.
- Doubt is not fear, and doubt is not evil.

When I posted that I was excited about the movie version of *Blue Like Jazz*, a Facebook friend commented, "I personally do not want to see a movie based on a heretical book. *Blue Like Jazz* is scripturally unsound and presents dangerous theology. It is coming out of the same circles as books like *Velvet Elvis* and *Love Wins*."

My friend and I then had a long conversation online about whether certain books or authors are good for Christians to read, since they might question traditional thinking. I explained that one of the things I enjoyed about *Blue Like Jazz* was that it asks a lot of questions that may make people uncomfortable. Jesus taught through stories and by asking questions. I like that. I like that *Blue Like Jazz* encouraged me to think and didn't just allow me to read my own opinions over and over again on paper. And I appreciate the courage of Christians who are willing to question in public, to let us know that we are not alone in our searching.

Of course, not everyone agrees with me on that. This is a common thread that I find in many Christian circles—the idea that questioning or doubting is inherently evil. That for some reason when we wonder about the mystery of an all-powerful God—or question the existence of someone so dangerous, amazing, terrible, lovely, and controversial—that it somehow ticks him off. That he is upset by limited human minds and sinful people trying to understand and make sense of something so outrageously difficult to believe.

I was recently at Mount Hermon, a great camp and conference center in the redwoods of California. There Mark Labberton, a pastor and professor, talked about how hard it was for his dad to believe. His dad was an intellectual—a deep thinker and a man who valued wonder. He had observed that the God most Christians talked about seemed rather small and explainable. This God certainly wasn't powerful enough and big enough to have created everything and set it in motion and have the ability to hold it all in tension. He had heard of a domesticated and tame God and thought that he couldn't believe in such a minimized being.

I think he had a point. If we feel God is so insecure that asking, questioning, and examining who the Bible says he is in light of all of the suffering in the world would upset him, then perhaps we don't understand the nature of God.

As a little child I often asked my mom and dad, "Why?" Why does this thing do that, and how does it work? These are normal questions for little kids to ask. Sometimes in exasperation, my parents would say, "Just because." Or even less satisfying, "Because I said so." But they weren't angry with me for wanting to know why something works or how it came to be. This is the nature of development and formation. Questions are a part of the journey. If life is a road, then questions are probably a cross between bumps and left turns. I haven't decided which. I don't believe asking honest questions along the way is right or wrong. It just is. Just because.

"Every time we give in to grace, we send fear packing."

BOB GOFF ON FACEBOOK, FEBRUARY 3, 2013

I think it is important that the motive behind the question be right. Sometimes we ask questions to inadvertently attack or accuse. When we hunger and thirst for God and we desire to know him and his ways, then our questions are more likely to be asked with a pure heart. For example, Job asked God questions, but he also was careful of what he said. He stood in awe of God and respected God's authority. Take a look through the book of Job and see how he asked God his questions and why he reacted the way he did.

Are you ever afraid to ask questions? Don't be. There are answers. They don't always come easily or quickly, but they are there. Some of the most Christlike people I've met and some of those most at peace with God and themselves are the ones who are able to live a life seeking, questioning, and wondering, while being sure of what they believe and in whom they believe at the deepest level.

WHAT IS REAL EVIL?

What about when you come face-to-face with real evil? What does it look like?

Evil is not the opposite of good. Let's get that straight.

It is difficult to define evil without sounding overly religious. *Evil! Sin! Demonic!* These are words that I mostly hear Christians use in a hyperbolic way, calling something *evil* that they may dislike, such as music with drums or a certain political stance. We need to stop using that word to describe things we disagree with or think are dumb. When we do that, we are watering down the meaning, and therefore our understanding, of evil.

If you've ever read *The Screwtape Letters* by C. S. Lewis, you know that, on the surface level, it's a book full of fictitious letters from a high-ranking demon to his subordinate—a demon-in-training, if you will. Toward the end of the book, I started to understand what Lewis seemed to be getting at. (I'm a bit slow . . . but I also read it when I was sixteen, so the hormones were probably blocking some of the thoughts.) The book seems to be more about the inner workings of the human mind and spirit than the actual demon-characters. It is about what makes us temptable, what enables us to do the wrong thing when we should do the right thing, and what allows us to justify doing wrong when we know what is right. Part of C. S. Lewis's point is that much of the work of demons is in distraction. Discombobulation.

> As this condition becomes more fully established, you will be gradually freed from the tiresome business of providing Pleasures as temptations. . . . You no longer need a good book, which he really likes, to keep him from his prayers or his work or his sleep; a column of advertisements in yesterday's paper will do. . . . You can make him do nothing at all for long periods. . . .
>
> You will say that these are very small sins; and doubtless, like all young tempters, you are anxious to be able to report spectacular wickedness. But do remember, the only thing that matters is the extent to which you separate the man from the Enemy. It does not matter how small the sins are, provided that their cumulative effect is to edge the man away from the Light and out into the Nothing. Murder is no better than cards if cards can do the trick. Indeed the safest road to Hell is the gradual one—the gentle slope, soft underfoot, without sudden turnings, without milestones, without signposts.[6]

Look over here! Now over there! Anywhere but at the heart of the matter. Evil is not the opposite of good. Evil is the perversion of good.

Who do we think of when we think of evil? Adolf Hitler. Everyone, without fail, seems to bring up Hitler when I ask about evil. He was a power-hungry bigot who caused the death of well over 11 million people.[7] Of course we think he was evil. But is being a leader evil? Is rising to power evil? Is having goals evil? "No, of course not," you say. Those are stupid questions.

The power Hitler had was not evil. The buildings he killed people in were not evil. The swastika was not evil. But Hitler and the Nazis *practiced evil* under the banner of the Third Reich. If a good man had written a book about his struggles in life (what Hitler called *Mein Kampf*) while he was in prison, had held no bitterness toward Jewish people, and hadn't wanted to kill Jews, gypsies, homosexuals, or prisoners of war, there would have been no Holocaust. Leadership is meant for good; it turned evil when Hitler abused his power to fulfill his own desires.

"Goodness is, so to speak, itself: badness is only spoiled goodness. And there must be something good first before it can be spoiled," C. S. Lewis said. "In order to be bad [a person] must have good things to want and then to pursue them in the wrong way: he must have impulses which were originally good in order to be able to pervert them."[8]

In other words, if evil were the opposite of good, it would want no good thing. Yet evil desires good things—but is wrong in the way it goes about getting and using them.

Sex was meant for good. But we pervert it and use it for our own selfish desires. Lust for someone you have not married. Rape. Incest. Evil.

What about politics? Power? Government? They are supposed to be used for good. But we see people take advantage of power and authority all the time. We see dictators and oppressive regimes enslave and misuse power to fulfill their own selfish goals. Evil.

If people take what is meant for good and try to shortcut their way to personal gain, if we hurt others to get what we want, if we abuse power, that is evil.

OVERCOME EVIL

Instead of fearing evil, we must overcome evil with good.[9] We must get closer to the only One who is good and bring his light to the dark places where evil flourishes. We must align our use of his creations with their intended good purposes.

The apostle Paul knew about overcoming evil. He was in prison. His life was probably in danger. But he reassured his friends, writing,

> I want you to know, my dear brothers and sisters, that everything that has happened to me here has helped to spread the Good News. For everyone here, including the whole palace guard, knows that I am in chains because of Christ. And because of my imprisonment, most of the believers here have gained confidence and boldly speak God's message *without fear*. . . .
>
> I will continue to rejoice. For I know that as you pray for me and the Spirit of Jesus Christ helps me, this will lead to my deliverance.
>
> For I fully expect and hope that I will never be ashamed, but that I will continue to be bold for Christ, as I have been in the past. And I trust that my life will bring honor to Christ, whether I live or die.

For to me, living means living for Christ, and dying is even better.

PHILIPPIANS 1:12-14, 18-21 (EMPHASIS ADDED)

To not fear death because we see it as a journey into the presence of God. To not fear anything in life because we know that the worst that can happen is death. To live for Christ. This is what chivalry is about. To understand the source of evil and overcome it with good. To refuse to allow fear to rule in our hearts.

Fear. It is hard to overcome. And we are only human. I sleep with a light on somewhere in the house most nights. I don't know why; I tell myself it's because it helps me sleep better. But I want to abolish fear from my life. And by the grace of God, I will not fear the darkness. I will not fear evil.

VIII

I WILL ALWAYS FOLLOW THE LAW UNLESS IT GOES AGAINST WHAT IS MORAL AND GOOD.

"Laws control the lesser [person]. . . .
Right conduct controls the greater one."

→ M A R K   T W A I N

AUDREY'S STORY

IT WAS AUDREY'S ELEVENTH BIRTHDAY. Her mother, the
Dutch baroness Ella van Heemstra, had purchased tickets for
the whole family to see a performance by a troupe of famous
English dancers. Audrey's mother had recently moved with
Audrey and her two brothers from England to the Netherlands
(sometimes referred to as Holland). Hitler and the Nazis were
on the move; nine months earlier they had invaded Poland. As
a result England and France declared war on Germany. Ella
thought Holland would be safer for her children since it was a
neutral country.

Audrey wore a new floor-length taffeta dress that rustled
when she moved. The gift from her mother was expensive, but
Audrey would be presenting flowers to the director at the end of
the performance. The director accepted little Audrey's flowers in
a hurry, as the English consul had advised the dance company to
get in and get out of Holland as quickly as possible.

The very next day, Nazis invaded the Netherlands. German
troops soon ravaged Arnhem, the city where Audrey lived. Her
family was allowed to stay in their home, but over the next ten
months, all of their valuable property was confiscated by Nazis.
Strict rations were imposed on food.

Audrey still had her father's English last name, Ruston. He
had left the family years earlier, shortly after meeting Hitler.

(He was later detained in England for distributing Nazi propaganda.) In an effort to protect her, Audrey's mother changed her daughter's name from Audrey Ruston to Edda van Heemstra.

Audrey watched her Jewish neighbors being herded like cattle into trucks, men into one, women into another, babies taken into yet another. "We did not yet know that they were going to their death," she recalls. "I remember, very sharply, one little boy standing with his parents on the platform, very pale, very blond, wearing a coat that was much too big for him, and he stepped on to the train. I was a child observing a child."[1]

Audrey feared, as many girls did, being picked up and taken to a military brothel. One day Audrey was walking alone in the street when three truckloads of armed soldiers stopped. The soldiers ordered several girls on the street to line up and climb into the truck. Audrey was one of them. As she rode in the truck, Audrey repeated the Lord's Prayer to herself in Dutch. The convoy stopped suddenly. Some of the soldiers got out, pulled a few Jewish people off another truck, and began beating them. Audrey later recounted, "I remember hearing the dull sound of a rifle butt hitting a man's face. And I jumped down, dropped to my knees and rolled under the truck. I then skittered out, hoping the driver would not notice me—and he didn't."[2]

It was Audrey's dream to "wear a tutu and dance at Covent Garden"[3] in London. Perhaps that dream was in her mind that day as she escaped the grasp of the Nazis.

Audrey was a child of war. She learned, as many do in hard times, to cope with the pain around her through art and creativity. She and some friends began holding secret dance shows as fund-raisers for the Dutch Resistance. After the performances, not a single person clapped, for fear of being discovered. "The best audience I ever had made not a single sound at the end of my performance," she said later.[4]

Sometimes resistance workers would attend these "black

performances," so called because they were performed in venues protected with blackout curtains and with little lighting. The resistance would give the young dancers money and messages to stuff into their shoes and secretly deliver to other resistance workers. Audrey and the other children risked their lives to save those resisting the Nazis.

"We saw young men put against the wall and shot and they'd close the street and then open it and you could pass by again," she says. "Don't discount anything awful you hear or read about the Nazis. It's worse than you could ever imagine."[5]

Years passed, and fifteen-year-old Audrey hung in the balance between life and death herself. Sick with jaundice, her legs and feet swollen from malnourishment, she found it almost impossible to walk up and down stairs.

Due to the Nazi rations, people were literally starving. The only way some survived was by frying tulip bulbs and baking grass into bread. Still the "Hunger Winter" of 1944–1945 was particularly harsh. So many people died of starvation that there were not enough coffins to bury them.[6]

In the spring of 1945, the fighting came closer and closer. Audrey and her family took refuge in the cellar as Nazi and Allied forces fought. But the morning of April 29 was unusually quiet. The shelling had stopped, as had the constant shooting. Audrey heard singing coming from above ground, and she recognized the smell of English cigarettes. Up the stairs they crept. Opening the front door, Audrey's family found themselves surrounded by English soldiers, all pointing guns at them.

"I screamed with happiness, seeing all these cocky figures with dirty bright faces, and shouted something in English," she says. "A cheer went up that they'd liberated an English girl."[7]

Once the war ended, Audrey went back to London and began formally training as a ballet dancer to pursue her dream. But her severe malnourishment during the war had taken a toll. She was never able to be the best dancer. Instead she became a chorus girl and earned a series of small parts in British films. Then she was picked for the lead role in the Broadway play *Gigi* at age twenty-two.

After the war, Audrey had changed her last name to Hepburn, which was her great-grandmother's maiden name and was linked to royalty. The actress went on to become Hollywood royalty.

HISTORY AND DISOBEDIENCE

I have a great respect for Audrey Hepburn—yes, she is one of the most beautiful women ever to have lived. But her character, her love for children and people who suffer, and her desire to create beauty in the midst of an ugly world are far more admirable than her classic sophistication. My admiration only grew when I learned of her heroic and unlawful acts when she was a child during the war.

Throughout history, there have been laws and decrees that have been immoral and have dictated a disrespect of life. Famously, many Nazi war criminals claimed to have just "followed orders"—but their orders were to torture and kill innocents. Audrey Hepburn was only one person of many who fought against powers that seemed impossible to face. But her story has changed my life.

Audrey and others like her have taught me that there may be times to stand up against the law and work to change it, refusing to cave in to what is socially acceptable. One of the Bible's most famous examples is when it was mandated that all the Hebrew baby boys under a certain age were to be killed in Egypt. Pharaoh's own daughter defied the law, picked up a Hebrew baby out of the water, and raised him as her son. World War II gives us many stories similar to Audrey's, stories of those who fought the Nazi regime in Germany and across Europe. In the United States during the civil rights movement, many people worked to end legal segregation, often disobeying the law to express their outrage and to bring about equality.

Around the world today, men and women work to protect the rights of others, fighting against legal genocide, the oppression of women, and the stifling of religious expression. In the last year, I've had dinner with two people who are engaged in these kinds of battles. One guy smuggles Bibles in and people out of places where it's illegal to do so, and another man has, by his own efforts, freed thousands of men, women, and children held in slavery. The incredible thing is, they are just like you and me.

People may be uncomfortable with this idea of civil disobedience. Some say that we should always obey every law, that we should always agree with leaders (which often seems to apply politically only when someone looks and sounds like us . . . interesting).

Not so long ago, in the 1960s in some parts of the southern United States, people had to consider whether they'd obey the law—or if they'd stand for equality of all people. There were very real consequences; lives were risked, and relationships were severed. In 1994, an estimated 800,000 people in Rwanda were killed in 100 days.[8] Where were the justice-loving people of the world in the midst of this?

I believe there is a time when we must take a stand, even against the law, when God's higher good is in conflict with the law of the land and the fate of humanity is in the balance. Genocide. Abortion. Exploitation of innocents. Abuse of women and children. All of which are government-endorsed in some parts of the world. And all, I believe, go against God's best for humanity and could possibly require disobeying the law.

THE MOST IMPORTANT LAW

So how do we know when it's okay to disobey the law—and when we *should* do so? What law could be higher than the laws our governments have put in place? Here's what Paul (the apostle) says:

> Let everyone be subject to the governing authorities, for there is no authority except that which God has established. The authorities that exist have been established by God. Consequently, whoever rebels against the authority is rebelling against what God has instituted, and those who do so will bring judgment on themselves. For rulers hold no terror for those who do right, but for those who do wrong. Do you want to be free from fear of the one in authority? Then do what is right and you will be commended. For the one in authority is God's servant for your good. But if you do wrong, be afraid, for rulers do not bear the sword for no reason. They are God's servants, agents of wrath to bring punishment on the wrongdoer. Therefore, it is necessary to submit to the authorities, not only because of possible punishment but also as a matter of conscience.
>
> This is also why you pay taxes, for the authorities are God's servants, who give their full time to

governing. Give to everyone what you owe them: If you owe taxes, pay taxes; if revenue, then revenue; if respect, then respect; if honor, then honor.

Let no debt remain outstanding, except the continuing debt to love one another, for whoever loves others has fulfilled the law. The commandments, "You shall not commit adultery," "You shall not murder," "You shall not steal," "You shall not covet," and whatever other command there may be, are summed up in this one command: "Love your neighbor as yourself." Love does no harm to a neighbor. Therefore love is the fulfillment of the law.

ROMANS 13:1-10, NIV

Love is the fulfillment of "the law." Here, the law would have been what the Hebrews lived by: the Law of Moses, as found in the Torah (the books which, in the Christian Bible, are called Genesis, Exodus, Leviticus, Numbers, and Deuteronomy). The Torah explains that this law was given by God for the protection of his people. They're principles of behavior that give us a framework in which to live and operate in morality and goodness. Do you know all the Ten Commandments without looking them up? I think I do. Give me a second. (This is your chance to write them down in the margins or on your hand.)

1. Don't worship other gods.
2. Don't make or worship any idols.
3. Don't misuse God's name with words or actions in vain (don't curse with it).
4. Keep a Sabbath day for rest. Keep it holy.

5. Honor your parents.
6. Don't kill people.
7. Don't cheat on your spouse.
8. Don't steal stuff.
9. Don't lie.
10. Don't be materialistic and want stuff that isn't yours.[9]

I think I got it.

Here's the deal: These are all great things—not killing people, not worshiping something you made out of wood, being satisfied with what you have. But this is not it. These rules are not their own fulfillment. For me, that's what a lot of the ideas in this book boil down to. All of the chapter titles make great rules, a great personal creed to follow. But if you follow rules for the sake of rules, you'll just find emptiness over and over again. If you attempt to obey the Ten Commandments, and even find some degree of success at toeing the line, you will still feel empty. I think that's what Jesus was getting at when he said, "Do not think that I have come to abolish the Law or the Prophets; I have not come to abolish them but to fulfill them."[10] All at the same time, he was upholding the law, pointing out its shortcomings, and calling his followers beyond it to so much more—to more of what we should do than what we shouldn't.

This book is about taking in the stories of people who either embodied these principles or failed. It's about learning from both groups. Storing it all up in our mind boxes and letting the information ruminate and brew a change of heart. It's about transformation that only comes by knowing Jesus well. The code of chivalry is an inside-out kind of deal—the creeds and promises and rules bring joy and fulfillment only when they overflow from a heart that has been changed by the scandalous love of Jesus—it's scandalous because he loves someone like me.

"BUT IT DOESN'T APPLY TO ME!"

Many of us would like to live without rules. Many people think the rules don't apply to them, that there is not a universal morality. I particularly like C. S. Lewis's point of view on this matter: "There is nothing indulgent about the Moral Law. It is as hard as nails. It tells you to do the straight thing and it does not seem to care how painful, or dangerous, or difficult it is to do."[11] Lewis basically makes the case that even young children know there is a right and wrong. And if there is an objective, universal understanding of morality, then there must be a Creator who set that standard in the hearts of humans. Through the understanding that we innately know some things are right and some things are wrong, we prove the existence of a God who instills that in us.[12]

We all know how we like to be treated. And we all like to be kept safe. We need to be law-abiding in order to prevent chaos. But some of us like to make concessions for little laws that we think are okay to break. We make up reasons why it's okay to steal music. And we joke about it. I can't tell you how many times I've left something somewhere for a couple of minutes only to return and find it had "walked away." We make up reasons why it's okay to take something that isn't ours.

It's important that we, as justice seekers, obey the law. Not look for ways to get around the law but live above reproach. Do we illegally download music? Rip off something that belongs to someone else? Sneak into a second movie so we can save money? If we want to have credibility, we must treat others as we wish to be treated. This is why being law-abiding is important. It's the Golden Rule. It's just the right thing to do. It does apply to me and to you. And no matter how much we like or dislike rules, we have to remember that our own interpretation of those regulations is not law. It's just opinion.

To my Christian friends: Why would we even make justifications for stealing music? Or anything else, for that matter?

I've heard people say, "Because they make plenty of money." (Not true; I have a lot of musician friends.) Even if they did, that music is their livelihood, and just as the T-shirt at the store isn't yours until you pay for it, so that song isn't yours until you've paid for it.

"Love is the final fight."

JOHN M. PERKINS

"Everyone else is doing it." "It's not that big of a deal." "At least I don't do it as much as that guy over there." (Do you hear how ridiculous these rationalizations sound? They're as bad as the middle schooler trying to find excuses to steal beer from his dad's minifridge. Or like one of the religious leaders Jesus chased out of the Temple with a handmade whip.)

We often excuse what we think our consciences will let us get away with. Things that we know are against the law or are wrong but don't seem as bad as other things. Or if there's something we really enjoy—even if it's harmful or illegal—we're eager to justify it. We will make excuses for what we want badly enough, directly related to how small it seems in relation to other sins.

For the record, I hate the word *sin*. It's used in the Bible and in Christian teachings, but not in the majority of culture, except sarcastically or to pander to Christians. I wonder about the definition of *sin* and why we use the term. Why people chose that word when they were translating the Bible. I thought I'd look it up: "the doctrine of sin." I found out that most often, the word translated *sin* in the Bible is the Greek word used to describe "missing the mark." I realize now that I've heard this before. Sin means to miss the mark, the standard, the bull's-eye. I say that I follow Jesus. If I'm trying to hit the mark he set, I can do nothing but fall short. I can, however, *try*. And I can seek to tuck in so closely to God that my longing will be to hit the mark and not make excuses.

WHEN TO DISOBEY THE LAW

I believe my generation may be called upon to disobey the law. I'm not talking only about American Christians and laws in the Western world. I'm talking about members of my generation around the globe and from all backgrounds.

If we are truly following Jesus, the day may come when we have to stand against the rule of law to follow God's best. If we lived in Rwanda during the genocide, would we have stood against the slaughter? If we had the chance to intervene with a government official who was selling children, would we step in and rescue the innocents? If we were required by law to report a pastor in our town who was forbidden to teach what he believed, would we do so, or would we disobey the law? If you were hiding a young slave who was "owned" by a rug loom operator and the local magistrate demanded you turn him over, would you?

Some of us in the Western world may feel like these situations are a bit far-fetched, or that they would never occur close to home. But all it would take is the passage of a few laws, a natural disaster of great enough magnitude, a large enough mob, and "good people" looking the other way, for these scenarios to be realized.

And when and if they are, how can we tell if we're justified in breaking the law? We should disobey the law when:

1. someone is being unfairly punished or oppressed,
2. someone's life is at stake, or
3. we would have to break a higher law to keep
   the laws of man.

I think discussions about these kinds of scenarios will happen more and more among my peers. We may find ourselves looking at history to consider those who have bravely stood against the status quo and risked their lives to protect others. Perhaps we can learn from their examples how we should live.

We are not above the law; we must commit to follow the law—unless it goes against what is moral and good. In some cases, that will be easy to determine. Others will be more difficult. We must weigh our actions prayerfully. And we must ensure that our actions are in keeping with God's law even while we break man's.

Martin Luther King Jr. was perhaps one of the greatest practitioners of civil disobedience, and he gives us this guidance: "How does one determine whether a law is just or unjust? A just law is a man made code that squares with the moral law or the law of God. An unjust law is a code that is out of harmony with the moral law. To put it in the terms of St. Thomas Aquinas: An unjust law is a human law that is not rooted in eternal law and natural law. Any law that uplifts human personality is just. Any law that degrades human personality is unjust."[13]

To discern this, we must agree that there is a higher right and wrong. We must ask ourselves how we would want to be treated on the other side of a suspected unjust law. We must commit ourselves fully to treating people how we want to be treated—how God wants us to treat them—even if that means breaking the laws of men. I honestly believe that if we followed the simple command—the greatest command in the law, according to Jesus—to love God with all our hearts and to "love our neighbor as ourselves"[14] to the fullest, we would do all the "right things," not because we had to, but because we wanted to.

The way of chivalry leads us to follow the law of the land and to break it when necessary to be obedient to God.

I WILL
LIVE AND
DIE WITH
HONOR.

"TO LIVE WILL BE AN AWFULLY BIG ADVENTURE."

PETER PAN IN HOOK

TO FEEL

BOBBING. Swaying. Leaning. Screeching.

Their last fight echoes in his mind. All the words he said and the ones he left unsaid.

Screeching. Puffing. Creaking.

The motion ceases—the external motion at least. This is his stop.

Getting out of the bus, the great, stinking people mover, he folds into the masses that funnel onto a descending dark staircase.

He flows numbly along with a crush of people. With arms pinned to his sides, he pushes only as much as necessary to reach his platform. If life is a river and people are fish, he feels like a rock, being gradually ground into sand with each ripple of the icy flow.

Just the day before, he had sat in the chamber of his therapist, Gary. The trip to Gary's office was an all-expenses-paid sort of thing, courtesy of Mother. *Gary thinks I'm really depressed; maybe he's right.*

Now the lurch of the train barely interrupts his thoughts. He rides this line to work every day. He gets on in the suburbs and eventually emerges in the bowels of the city in which he works. His arms are the hands of a clock and his head, a statue. His eyes don't normally rove, but today is different. Today he sees hurt all around. *Is it just me, or do the clouds cry when I've run out of tears?*

Gary told him about the five stages of grief: denial, anger, bargaining, depression, and acceptance. *I wonder if it's possible to feel the first four all at once*, he thinks as part of a flurry of thoughts.

Years of bargaining at his work have made him a hard negotiator, but you cannot negotiate with life—or death.

He is aware and attentive. He knows pain when he sees it. He can recognize the look of it in someone's eyes. In the jerk of a knee. The weighted shuffle of a walk. He has felt it himself. He's only human; of course he has. Like any other bipedal being directed by the electrical currents—storms even—of the cerebral cortex, he has felt pain. It has chastened him, berated him, taught him what to avoid and flee . . . but sometimes it's not so simple. He loved her. He still does.

He looks out the window of the speeding bullet to watch the scenery turn wet and hot as it melts and the world becomes a tube of stone.

The blur gives way eventually to more walking. Bumping. Jostling.

Two blocks later, he rides an elevator to the upper canopy of the concrete jungle.

But the higher he climbs, the lower he feels. This work—*his* work—pulled him away from her in her time of greatest need. He can't change the past.

Yet, he senses a muted glimmer within. Does it feel like change? Or can it change him? He feels what he hasn't felt for so long. More pain, yes, but . . . purpose, perhaps. He knows he can change.

LIFE AND PAIN

Of the five senses—sight, smell, sound, taste, and touch—
I think the one most underappreciated is touch. With vivid
descriptions, we tell friends about the amazing vistas we saw
on a trip; we stop in our tracks outside a bakery to inhale the
aroma of freshly baked bread; we spend hours listening to our
favorite music; and several times a day we seek out meals and
snacks based on the flavors we enjoy. But touch usually doesn't
get quite as much attention. Maybe it's because there's a dark
side of touch. No, I'm not talking about any kind of forbidden
or sexual touching.

I'm talking about pain.

Because we have the physical ability to feel, we have the
ability to experience pain. And isn't it interesting that we also
describe nonphysical, or emotional, discomfort with the same
word—*pain*? The two are so closely related that they often seem
as one.

The way we deal with the pain in our lives is directly propor-
tional to the way we live with honor—or without it.

Most of us can't remember the first time we scraped our
knee. Or the first time we accidentally burned our little fingers
or tongues, overeager to plunge some freshly foraged delight
into our mouths. Little pains are a part of life. And sometimes
it's not enough to tell a kid not to touch the stovetop or mess
with fire ants or play with broken glass. Pain tells us something.
It has meaning.

If you were to ask what pain *means*, a doctor might tell you
that pain is a warning that something is wrong, that some part
of your body needs attention. A scientist might tell you that

pain is a reason, a signal *not* to do what you just did. In essence, it lets us know when we are doing something wrong or danger-ous . . . most of the time. But as a deep feeler, I'm inclined to think that maybe pain is not as simple as that. Maybe there's a greater, deeper purpose.

Have you ever missed someone so much that your heart outweighed the rest of you and your arms ached heavily for the lack of an embrace? Have you ever lost somebody, and the pain transcended the emotion until you felt it in your body? It hurts. Is it not enough to be apart? Is it *not enough* that what was once in existence only exists in memory? Why must pain linger like a bitter aftertaste or an ache in our chests that stalls our hearts and burns our eyes and makes us want to strike at everything but won't even let us move? *What good is pain?*

PERSPECTIVES ON PAIN

I was talking to my friend Jordan about all this. I knew Jordan when I was really young; we played on a soccer team that my dad coached. We've reconnected since then. Jordan's a really great art-ist, and he's a thinker. We were talking about the purpose, rather than the problem, of pain and how life includes pain, not just pleasure. I'd love for you to eavesdrop on the conversation:

> **Jordan:** Pain isn't a transaction. You're not entitled to something because of your pain. People sometimes think they deserve compensation because they went through something terrible. So they expect others— even people who had nothing to do with their pain— to kind of cater to them because of what happened to them in the past.

I had a friend whose house was destroyed in a natural disaster before I knew him. Whenever people brought up something bad that had happened to them, this guy would bring up his past pain, usually with a tone of "Oh, this horrible thing happened to *me*, so you should get over your pain." It was almost like he was saying, "You don't deserve to whine, even though I do all the time." He acted as though his pain from the past trumped the pain of everyone he knew. As though his experience deserved the spotlight and no one else should try to push him out of it. He acted like he was entitled to have a monopoly on—

Zach: People's pity?

Jordan: Exactly.

Zach: It seems so much healthier when people who have gone through pain act more sympathetic to others who are hurting instead of acting like, "My pain was worse than yours." I guess pain can either make you more understanding of everyone else or make you think that you are better than other people.

Jordan: Maybe it's not always thinking you're better than; sometimes people act like they demand sympathy or compassion from other people because they've had it rough.

Zach: So one type of pain comes when something is taken away from you; and people feel like they're owed something in return, like sympathy or pity, at least. That's treating pain as a transaction. But there's a flip side when people act like pain is a result of something.

Jordan: Right. That's treating pain like a consequence.

But pain may not always be a result of something we've done.

Zach: Sure, sometimes we get sick because there's disease—not because we've made a bad decision. Sometimes we take all the necessary precautions, and bad stuff still happens to us. It's not necessarily because we did something wrong, but because the world is screwed up.

Jordan: I think there's definitely pain that is part of the plan that God has for you. Pain can be used to shape you and how you view yourself and other people. I don't say, "God has a plan" as a feel-good kind of statement. That phrase often gets misused.

Zach: Yeah, people can say, "God has a plan" flippantly. We just throw it at people without listening to them and walking through the pain with them because we don't know what else to say. But it would be totally insensitive if I said that to someone who just lost a child. It'd be more about trying to make myself feel better or less confused than really helping that person.

Jordan: Yeah, it's hard enough to make sense of our own pain, much less someone else's. We've got to avoid sounding like, "The Creator of the universe must want you to be in terrible pain and agony at this point. But don't worry; it's God's plan. That's just how it is!"

Zach: Exactly. Especially in situations we've never been through. I have no idea how it feels to lose an immediate family member. But I can see how specific instances, like a terrible breakup or moving from one place to another where I don't know anyone, have shaped me. Sometimes for better, sometimes for worse, depending how I've chosen to deal with it. Hopefully my own experiences with pain give me more compassion for other people who are suffering.

My friends often teach me things. From this conversation with Jordan I gained a few takeaways:

1. Pain is not a transaction. Just because I've experienced it doesn't mean I'm entitled to something else in return. *I'll take this pain, but I want your admiration and undying sympathy in return* is the wrong attitude.

2. Our experience with pain doesn't give us permission to be jerks; we don't need to compare our past pain with someone else's in order to prove ours is or was worse. That can cause us to seem unsympathetic and self-centered to those around us. And that's not an honorable way to live.

3. Pain is a gift that can help direct our path. Just as physical pain tells us when to remove our hand from a pan so it doesn't get burned, emotional pain can cause us to seek God's direction so we don't make the same mistakes twice, which can hurt others as well as ourselves. In this case, pain is a consequence of our actions, not a transaction. In some cases, pain isn't a direct consequence of anything we've done, but we can still let God use it to shape us.

Pain has a reason. "[Pain] removes the veil; it plants the flag of truth within the fortress of a rebel soul."[1] When breaking, we can choose not to be broken. Pain is necessary. Everything is for a reason.

Only to the masochist and the sadist is pain actually enjoyable. Humanity, as a whole, tries to avoid pain at any cost. But what if we recognized pain as redemptive? Not as a friend, not as an enemy, but as a teacher? Pain, shock, repercussions . . . they teach us something. Either they reveal truth, or they show us what not to do. Either way, feeling is worth it. Pain is evidence we are alive.

As C. S. Lewis said in *The Problem of Pain*, "God whispers to us in our pleasures, speaks in our conscience, but shouts in our pains: it is His megaphone to rouse a deaf world."[2]

Part of living in this temporary world involves pleasure and pain. One we love. The other, we often despise. But being fully alive means we need to accept pain and allow it to teach us—even when we can't fully understand it.

> **"How we spend our days is, of course, how we spend our lives."**
>
> ANNIE DILLARD, *THE WRITING LIFE*

The reason I took so much time to talk about pain as a part of living with honor is that, for many of us, our painful times define us. We often remember more acutely the times of pain than the times of pleasure. How we let those difficult times affect us can ultimately define our character.

LIVING WITH HONOR AND FINDING JOY

Do we believe that pain can change us for the better; that hope can come from hardship? That is what it ultimately comes down to.

If we believe that this world is not all there is, then we should live with hope and joy for something more. In the midst of pain and definitely in the midst of mundane, everyday hassles, we should be filled with wonder. Even when things are tough, we can choose to live with our eyes wide open like a little child discovering something for the first time.

Most of the time, we go through life without really embracing it. We have these wonderful things called senses, yet we often go through entire days without being really cognizant of them. We go through our routine, not noticing textures, smells, sights, or even the people who are in our path.

"We're all dying—but are we really living?" said my friend's mom, Minnie. She knew what she was talking about. She was approaching the end of her battle with cancer. Although her life was ending, she chose to continue investing in people. With the little energy she had, she encouraged others who were living with cancer. She reached out to students who were friends of her son. She purposefully chose to use the days she had left to stay connected with the people she loved.

Rather than just ticking off days and passing time, living with honor requires that we view each day as a gift. As though something amazing is awaiting us. Living expectantly.

We live with honor by investing our time well. By investing in others. By taking advantage of opportunities we have and discovering the wonder of all it takes for our lives to continue— our breathing, our pulse, our senses. By being fully alive. A mysterious and magical reality: we are walking around in human form with a body, mind, and spirit—visitors here for a short time with an eternal destination. We must seize the moments we have in this temporary home and not waste them.

God is the Creator, the giver of life. And yet, even we Jesus followers have become increasingly calloused about life, and maybe even cruel. According to Annie Dillard, "Cruelty is a mystery, and the waste of pain."[3] As we learn to respect the life giver and respect ourselves, we will be compelled to respect all those he created—those with faces and names next to us in everyday life as well as those far away on the other end of causes we care about. As a generation who has taken up the cause of justice, nothing less should be expected.

SUICIDE IS NOT AN HONORABLE DEATH

Suicide is the third leading cause of death among fifteen to twenty-four year olds.[4] But when we live for something—Someone— we must realize that our lives are not our own to take. It is not bravery to choose to take your life. You are deciding that anything you could offer to the world or could do to possibly change the world is not worth the pain you're going through. It's deciding that any people you are close to or could possibly grow close to are not worth staying alive for. You have far too much left to do on this earth to rob anyone of your life.

One of the reasons many young people think suicide is a reasonable solution to our problems is that we haven't been around long enough to put the pain in context. We see only what's right in front of us or immediately behind us. So we look at a breakup or someone's mockery or our own depression, and we see the immediate future alone, full of heartache. We have been embarrassed or abused by others and envision only a life stigmatized by those scars, as if that's all people will ever see when they look at us.

But throughout time, people have been hurt, humiliated, and misused and have refused to let the pain, or the persecutors, win. They stood up, took the next step, and started to move forward with life.

Although everyone goes through hard times, sometimes pain morphs into true depression. That kind of despair is too big a burden for anyone to carry alone. If you're struggling with depression or thoughts of suicide, I encourage you to seek help from a trusted family member or teacher. Or call the National Suicide Prevention Hotline at 1-800-273-TALK (8255) to speak with a trained counselor.

But suicide isn't the only dishonorable death. There are other causes that take the lives of far too many people. Friends die from drug overdoses and DUI accidents because they think they are invincible. Carelessness and stupidity are not honorable causes of death.

I truly believe God has a purpose for our lives. None of us are here by accident. God will give us the strength to make it through whatever pain we're facing. He can bring healing and good out of our worst darkness. There's a bigger picture than our immediate suffering. It's all part of God restoring us—our lives, our relationships, our world, and ultimately his entire creation, which has been broken. Don't give up. There's more. There's better. Keep living your life and investing in the lives of others. That's what chivalry is all about.

LIVING WITH PURPOSE

Living with honor requires—maybe even enables—us to hold our heads up and say, "My past will *not* define me! I will take control of my future, or at least all the decisions that I am given to manage, and I will live the best life I can from this point forward."

When you get discouraged, think of people whose embarrassment or pain could have caused them to give up. Even when they made repeated, stupid, bona fide mistakes—the kind the whole world finds out about—they kept going. Former presidents and professional athletes have been caught in scandals that would embarrass them for the rest of their lives. But they chose to learn from the pain of the moment and focus ahead on what the rest of their lives could be, should be. True, some celebrities have simply put a spin on mistakes they've been caught in without truly learning from them. But others have learned one step at a time, one day at a time, and refocused on where to go from there.

That, my friend, is an honorable way to face our tragedies, heartbreaks, pains, and embarrassments. Not to let them overcome or define us, but to commit to living with integrity, honesty, and dignity, so that the brushstrokes of our future begin to cover over the past and paint a beautiful new picture of who we really are.

We aren't just sleepwalking through life. We are wide-awake, living with the purpose of sharing perfect love with the world around us. Your quest in life—whatever it may be—is the unique way you fulfill this purpose.

Just as we must choose to overcome our pain and let it make us stronger, we must make the most of the other resources we are given. Taking care of our bodies, not abusing these physical "tents" we live in, avoiding harmful substances—these are also elements of living with honor. Hurting our bodies purposefully through self-injury and harmful habits, including eating disorders, doesn't demonstrate a life well lived. It doesn't show a gratefulness for this gift we have been given.

I know the pain can be overwhelming. I know it can feel so all-consuming that there's no way out. And if you struggle with self-injury or an eating disorder, you're not alone. Please seek out help and consider calling the hotline mentioned previously. Please talk to someone who can give you help and support.

But if we believe that we are created in the image of God, then our bodies are meant to be a reflection of his creativity and care. That's their original wondrous design before stuff on earth might have messed up how we see them. Choose to take care of yourself—you are here for such a short time. Make a commitment to honor others with your words and actions. Choose to let pain and disappointment teach you. Rather than masking your pain, or engaging in unhealthy and destructive behaviors, talk with people you trust. Share your struggles with them. Ask them to walk with you as you try to understand what you can learn through tough or even tragic times. Ask God to show you how to demonstrate grace to yourself.

In times of struggle, depression, or doubt, it can really help to see your role in the world by helping someone else. Volunteer, tutor, give your time in a way that makes a difference for others and allows you some breathing room from your own troubles.

The same is true even if you're not dealing with pain right now. Be glad you're not, but open your eyes to the people around you who are hurting. Apply the lessons you've learned from your pain. Share compassion. Offer encouragement—not through empty words, but through friendship, relationship, and support. Live out the kind of grace you wish you had in your darkest moments. You can be a source of hope and light in someone's worst darkness.

Live with honor and treat others with honor. Invest your life in such a way that upon your honorable death you will have left a positive mark on the earth. Then you will be able to pass with honor, entering into the realization of hope you've been expecting all your life.

X

I Will
Never Abandon
My Quest.

"Do not grow weary of doing good."

2 Thessalonians 3:13, NASB

SIR GARETH'S QUEST

ONE MORNING IN THE COURT OF KING ARTHUR, the knights of
the Round Table were feasting together when a maiden ran into
the hall. "My king," she cried, "how can you sit there and feast
when evil runs rampant through your kingdom?"

The king rose and replied, "Be assured, maiden, that none of
us will rest when there are wrongs to be righted and evil to be
vanquished. What is your name? And what is your need?"

"My name is Lady Lynette. I have come to beg the service of
Sir Lancelot to free my sister, Lady Lyonors, who is being held
prisoner by four evil knights. Three of the knights—Morning
Star, Noonday Sun, and Evening Star—guard the only path to
the Castle Perilous. And the fourth, Night Star, is guarding
my sister."

"Fair Lynette," said Arthur, "the Order of the Round Table
exists only to uphold justice. Every one of my brave knights would
eagerly go to the rescue of your sister. Take cheer, for none seek
our aid in vain."

While the king was deciding which of his knights to send
on the quest, the kitchen boy approached. The lad was a young
peasant, dressed in little more than sacks. He was known as
Fair Hands. A year earlier, this young man had come to the king
asking for three things: first, that he be permitted to serve for
one year in Arthur's kitchen, working only for food and drink.

After he completed this commitment, he would present his other two requests. He was strong and tall and carried himself like a person of noble birth even though his position betrayed him. He was placed under the authority of Sir Kay who seemed to be quite jealous of the young man. He gave him the title of Fair Hands because he had large, pale hands—the hands of a boy who had not had to work a day in his life. Fair Hands had, however, found good friends in Sir Lancelot and Sir Gawain, two of the most decorated knights of the Round Table.

"What would you ask of me?" said King Arthur to Fair Hands.

"I have come to thank you, my king, for the sustenance and shelter you have granted to me these past twelve months. You will recall that after a year's time, I was to come to you again with two more requests. The first is that I might have the honor of going to rescue this maiden's sister. The second, that I may be knighted after I complete my quest."

The king smiled. "Your requests shall be granted, for you have truly served me well."

What King Arthur did not know was that Fair Hands's real name was Gareth. He was the son of a great king who had once been an enemy of Arthur and had done him a great wrong. When Prince Gareth had told his mother, a queen, that he wanted to become a knight, she released him to his journey under the condition that his real name would not be known, forcing him to become a servant until he had proved his worthiness.

When Lynette heard Fair Hands's requests, she was irate. "I came to you asking for the aid of the worthy Sir Lancelot—a truly noble knight who has proven himself on and off the battlefield to be the best defender and a most honorable man. But you offer me a kitchen boy! Do you care so little about your subjects that you send a boy to do a knight's job?" Then she stormed from the hall, mounted her horse, and rode from the castle grounds.

Gareth was quickly outfitted with a horse and armor. Quietly the king asked Sir Lancelot to follow the boy he still knew as Fair Hands, to look after him from a distance.

Gareth looked every inch a knight, transforming into his true strength and power as he rode out to accomplish his quest. When he eventually caught up with Lynette, she said with disdain, "Do not come near me! You still smell of lard and smoked meat."

"My lady," Gareth calmly replied, "King Arthur has appointed me to be your humble protector, and I will not quit until I have rescued your sister or have died in the effort." His reply made her even angrier, and she rode her horse into the forest. Gareth again chased after her.

It was nearly dusk when Gareth came upon Lynette. Her face was haggard, and her horse looked equally exhausted. Gareth suggested they stop for the night, and despite her pride, Lady Lynette agreed.

Gareth built up a fire and began roasting some meat and potatoes. Lynette's stomach growled. "Are you hungry, my lady?" asked Gareth.

"Not in the least," said Lynette, turning away. "Besides, I will not sit and eat beside a mere kitchen boy."

"Very well, my lady." So Gareth took his portion of the meal and walked away from the fire, allowing Lady Lynette to sit and eat by herself.

When he returned and set up a tent, she protested against "sleeping under that filthy rag." Gareth explained, "It is either the tent or nothing, my lady. But if you prefer to sleep under the stars as I do . . ." At that she scurried into the tent and said nothing more.

The following morning, they set out again. Gareth said, "Lead the way, and I will follow."

Lynette said bitterly, "I will no longer flee from you, but if you value your life, you will go no farther. For nearby there is a knight who will surely send you to your grave."

Prince Gareth only smiled. As they rode, she constantly mocked him, and yet he remained ever silent and long-suffering. Soon they neared a dark forest, and the path became a small bridge suspended over a rushing river. Just on the edge of the far bank, they saw a tent pitched in a clearing. The golden silk of the fabric bathed the surrounding trees with golden light. Emerging from the peak of the tent was a crimson flag waving gallantly in the breeze. An unarmed knight emerged and shouted to Lynette, "Maiden! Is this the knight of the Round Table you have brought with you to compel me to allow you passage?"

"Oh, no, Sir Morning Star," replied Lynette. "King Arthur thinks you to be of such little threat that he has sent a mere kitchen boy in the stead of a knight."

Sir Morning Star donned armor as blue as the sky and took up a blue shield engraved with a brilliant morning star. As Gareth watched, Lynette taunted him, "Don't just sit there shaking with fear. There is still time for you to run away before the knight mounts his horse."

"Maid Lynette," replied Prince Gareth, "I would rather fight one hundred men than have you believe me a coward."

A moment later both men lowered their spears and charged toward each other across the bridge. Each took careful aim, making full contact with the other's shield. Both men were knocked off their horses and onto the bridge. Quickly they rose, continuing to battle on foot. Gareth's shield was sliced in half. But with a mighty downward swing, Gareth thrust his sword through his enemy's breastplate, knocking him down. He placed his foot upon his opponent's chest and held his sword to Sir Morning Star's throat. "I yield! I yield!" cried the knight.

Gareth sheathed his sword and sent the defeated knight to King Arthur's court, telling him to beg the king's forgiveness and to relay the news that the kitchen boy had sent him. Gareth claimed Morning Star's shield as a replacement for his own.

As they rode on, Lynette said, "Kitchen boy, it almost seemed as if the smell of grease faded a bit when you were fighting that villainous knight on the bridge. But I need to warn you: we are coming upon a knight who could kill you blindfolded. He is one of the brothers of Sir Morning Star."

Gareth only said, "My duty is to protect you, and protect you I shall."

They soon came to a bend in the river, where the water became shallower but very fast moving. Across the shallows, seated on a horse painted blood-red, they saw Morning Star's brother, Noonday Sun, furnished with shining, mirrored armor.

"Who are you? And how dare you trespass on my property?" he shouted.

"He is only a kitchen boy," said Lynette. "But he defeated your brother by chance, and now he has come thinking he can best you!"

Seeing that Gareth held his brother's shield, Noonday Sun lowered his visor and forced his horse into the river where Gareth met him halfway. Horses reared and twisted as the knights swung their swords amidst the spray, battering each other with glancing blows. Suddenly Noonday Sun bludgeoned Gareth with his shield. It was all the prince could do to stay upon the horse as his sword dropped into the rushing river. Sensing victory, Noonday Sun moved to deliver the final blow, but his horse lost its footing. Noonday Sun struck his head sharply on his horse's neck as the animal reared and was thrown from the beast. The river flowed red with blood as Noonday Sun lay motionless with his face in the water. Gareth jumped from his horse to collect his sword. Unwilling to let his enemy drown, he dragged the battered opponent to safety. As the knight revived, Gareth told him, "Go to King Arthur and tell him the kitchen boy sent you."

Turning to Lynette, Gareth said, "Lead, and I will follow."
Lynette barely acknowledged him, but Gareth did not complain.

An hour later they came to another bridge. Lynette pointed
across the river. There stood the third brother, Evening Star.
Upon seeing that Gareth held Morning Star's shield, Evening
Star shouted, "Hello, brother star! Have you slain the maiden's
champion?"

"He is no brother of yours, false knight," said Lynette. "Yet he
is a star, sent by King Arthur. He has crushed your brothers and
has come for you!"

The two knights charged at each other on foot and fought
with stunning intensity. Evening Star seemed as huge and as
strong as an ox. Gareth kept thinking he had tired his opponent
out, but time and again, Evening Star seemed to catch another
wind. As Gareth's heart began to fail him, Lynette called out,
"Well done, kitchen boy! You are truly as brave and strong as any
knight of the Round Table!"

Gareth felt courage bubble up like a spring within his chest.
With renewed strength, he hacked at his enemy's armor.
Roaring, Evening Star grabbed Gareth, pinning him to the bridge.
With all the strength he had left, Gareth twisted his body, plunging both men into the river. Gareth landed on top of Evening Star,
knocking him unconscious. Staggering out of the water, Gareth
left his opponent to sink or swim.

When he had remounted his horse, Gareth said to Lady
Lynette once more, "Lead, and I will follow."

"No," the maiden answered. "Henceforth, you shall ride
next to me, not behind me. I have wronged you with my words.
Berated you. Belittled you. And I am sorry—"

"My lady," interrupted Gareth, "your jokes and jibes are what
gave me strength. But now, how much stronger will I be, since
you have spoken such sweet words to me. Not even Lancelot
could defeat me now!"

At that very moment, Sir Lancelot rode around the bend. His shield was covered so he wouldn't be identified. Seeing Gareth with Morning Star's shield, Lancelot cried, "Villain, I shall lay you low and avenge my friend!"

Lancelot charged and caught Gareth a blow on his shield, sending him to the ground. Landing on his backside, Gareth couldn't help but laugh. Lancelot circled back around and said, "How dare you laugh, Morning Star?"

"I am not Morning Star, Sir Knight. My name is Gareth. I laugh to think that I, the son of a king and recent victor on that bridge, should be bested by an unknown knight!"

Recognizing his friend's voice and overjoyed that he was alive, Lancelot dismounted and helped Gareth up.

The three travelers sat down and talked about their journey, Lynette praising Gareth's battle prowess. Lancelot uncovered his shield and gave it to Gareth, bidding him farewell and Godspeed on the completion of his mission. Gareth accepted the generous gift, and he and Lynette rode off side by side toward the end of their quest.

They rode through the night, pausing once for a long rest. Shortly after they had remounted their horses, the Castle Perilous came into view through the early morning haze. Suddenly, Lynette reached over and clung to Gareth's shield with a look of panic in her eyes. "Gareth, return this shield to Lancelot," she pleaded. "I would bite off my mocking tongue, but I couldn't forgive myself if something happened to you. He should be the one to fight. You are a hero, but you are not a miracle worker!"

"Be that as it may, I would defeat this last foe and free your sister, or die in the act."

As they drew near the castle, they saw a huge black tent nearby. In front of it, on a crooked stick driven into the ground, hung a large, black horn. Before Lynette could stop him, Gareth grabbed the horn and blew into it.

They heard footsteps and looked up to see Lady Lyonors, Lynette's sister, peering out through the battlement atop the castle. Lyonors waved to Gareth, who blew the horn again. At this, a monstrous creature emerged from the tent, clad in black furs and oily black armor, riding a steed the color of charcoal. On his armor was painted the bones of a skeleton, and his helmet was topped not with a plume but with a human skull. From each side of the helmet stuck a massive antler, stained black with dried blood. The knight's name was Night Star.

Gareth's steed neighed loudly, which startled the black horse. The dark beast reared and bolted, throwing his master heavily to the ground and breaking off one of the antlers. Night Star rose slowly and struggled to lift his massive broadsword. Gareth leapt from his horse and delivered one mighty stroke, splitting through his foe's shield. Night Star fell flat on his back. Gareth yanked off his enemy's helmet, prepared to end the quest with a fatal blow. He was shocked to discover not the face of the Grim Reaper but that of a terrified teenage boy.

"Spare me, sir! My brothers made me don this disguise, thinking that no one would want to fight such a frightening-looking figure."

After sending the boy to meet with his brothers at King Arthur's castle, Gareth and Lynette enjoyed a festive reunion with Lady Lyonors. And Lynette was exceedingly proud of her kitchen-boy knight.

Then sprang the happier day from underground;
And Lady Lyonors and her house, with dance
And revel and song, made merry over Death,
As being after all their foolish fears

And horrors only proven a blooming boy.
So large mirth lived, and Gareth won the quest.[1]

THE HUMBLE BEGINNINGS OF A NOBLE QUEST

These principles of chivalry, this code of the knights—they're all very countercultural. Even this last part—never abandoning our quest—forces us to do some serious introspection. We have to ask ourselves:

What do I do when I want to give up?
What will give me the strength to keep going?
Is persevering always the right thing to do?

These are not questions we ask every day. Typically it's one foot in front of the other without really thinking through our long-term goals and the barriers to reaching them. Sometimes taking a little inventory—seeing where we really are—helps us recalibrate or recommit ourselves to reaching our goals.

We all have a purpose—to share love with those around us. Your quest is simply the unique way you do that, investing your talents and following your passions.

To what extremes are you willing to go to accomplish your dreams? Gareth put himself in the position of a lowly servant so he could be near the leaders he wanted to get to know, those he wanted to serve alongside in a different, bigger way. Would you volunteer in the mail room or on the grounds crew of a company that you really wanted to work for? Would it be worth it to you to be thought of as a peon?

I looked up *peon* on UrbanDictionary.com. (It's not a legitimate dictionary, in case you were wondering.) It is defined as someone who is "one social level below serfs, untouchables, and freshmen."[2] Which is funny, but also kind of insightful. Starting at what we perceive to be the bottom can feel like we're floating around somewhere in a strata of subhumanity, especially when we would rather be doing the "real work" somewhere higher up. We can feel worthless (or worth little) when we're in a position many perceive as lowly.

When someone is new to a job—whether at a fast-food restaurant, a corporation, or even on a professional sports team—that worker is often placed at the bottom rung of the employee ladder. In many settings, the person who's newest (just beginning his or her quest) gets the worst jobs, the ones nobody else wants. In fast food, that might be cleaning the fryer, which I understand is a nasty, greasy endeavor that requires draining and disposing of the old grease, removing several days' worth of gunk and junk from cooking, and refilling the machine with new grease. Do you think the senior-level cook does this? The head chef? Not likely. The newest, or youngest, person gets this delightful job.

> **"However difficult the moment, however frustrating the hour, it will not be long, because 'truth crushed to earth will rise again.'"**
>
> DR. MARTIN LUTHER KING JR.

In a corporation, the new guy or gal is the one asked to scan and file five years' worth of old newsletter articles or run out to fill up the boss's car with gas.

Even in the National Football League, rookies are compelled to carry the veterans' helmets and shoulder pads off the practice field and back to the locker room—sometimes six or eight sets of pads at once. They may also be ordered to sing for their meals, standing up on a chair in the dining room and belting out a tune before they can eat.

For some, the experience can be so humbling—or worse, humiliating—that they bail out. They quit. They believe that the end result, or the eventual payback of a rewarding job, is not worth the initial discomfort. And maybe it really isn't. But the only one who can decide is the person on the mission.

If your only goal is to make money to pay for clothing, gas, or entertainment, you may decide it's not worth it to go home from work coated with grease every day. There are other ways to make money. But if your goal is to learn the business, rise through the ranks, and one day manage or run your own restaurant, you may willingly endure uncomfortable or humbling circumstances in order to complete your quest. Maybe you even just want to learn something in your lowly position that will help you later.

The same is true in the corporate world or in professional sports. You may think that football players' rewards are great enough to warrant any level of temporary humiliation or even hazing. I guess that depends upon what you value, what you hope and dream for, what you want to accomplish in life.

For many of us, making millions of dollars playing a game sounds like an excellent career path—who wouldn't want that? But since so few players actually make it to the NFL, it's probably more realistic to think of another career that would be equally rewarding and fulfilling. In other words, if we can't make millions playing football, what would we like to be doing in our lives, with our lives, that would be rewarding and fulfilling?

A man I've referred to most of my life as Uncle Ted often talks about "emotional wages." What he means is that sometimes we may not see immediate financial gain as we do our jobs or complete our assignments. Instead, we may hear about a life we've touched or a person we've helped. Those are emotional wages. And when we take note of the things that bring us joy and satisfaction, particularly the way our work affects other people, we can gain insight into what drives us, what motivates us, and what we may actually be wired by our Creator to do with our lives. Of course, there may be times when we won't see any rewards—emotional or financial—this side of eternity. But our reputations should identify us as hardworking and dedicated people.

The character Gareth seemed completely hardwired to be a knight of the Round Table. He was so committed to knighthood that he was willing to earn his way there. He decided to start at the bottom of the ladder, in a lowly position, because he saw it as a means to an end—the way to accomplish his quest. He viewed humility, even brutal treatment by Lynette, as worthwhile because it was temporary. He believed he would one day accomplish his goals, so he didn't let a humble beginning discourage him and drive him to quit.

PASSION MAKES THE DIFFERENCE

Many people want to help out of the goodness of their hearts when they hear of the significant needs of others—the poor, the hungry, the oppressed, or enslaved. I'm often asked, "What can I do?"

That is the exact question I asked my parents when I was twelve, when I was first learning about modern-day slavery.

I wanted to contribute my twelve-year-old energy to helping others get out of slavery and find freedom. I didn't think, *Oh no, I'm too young to do anything.* I thought, *This is wrong—I have to do something.*

At first, people tried to rein me in. I heard from my parents and others, "Zach, you're only twelve. There's nothing you can do except pray for the victims and the rescuers. You can't go to other parts of the world and actually free slaves." But when my parents saw that I wasn't giving up, they helped me find another way to accomplish my quest.

That's when I came up with the idea to raise money to send more rescuers out into the world to free slaves. I called it Loose Change to Loosen Chains, and it continues today on school campuses around the world. The campaign has raised over a million dollars to fund freedom efforts. It wasn't exactly a brilliant or revolutionary idea. It was a fund-raiser with an admittedly cheesy name, but people caught the passion.

Many young people today want to get from A to Z in one step. You might have desires to do all kinds of things like play in the NBA or be a rock star or be a politician. (May God have mercy on your soul.)

But so many dreams in life take time, perseverance, and a number of steps to complete. Great pianists usually have to take years of lessons, learn how to read music flawlessly, practice for hours each day, and record themselves over and over. Often, they have to be mentored as well. Yet many kids give up on piano lessons after a few lessons because they don't see the progress they want. That's what I did with piano lessons. I didn't care enough about playing classical pieces perfectly to want to put myself through all of that. Laziness played a big part in it, but being a piano virtuoso just wasn't something I was passionate about.

If you want to do *something* significant, if you want to make a difference, if you're tired of being bored, you're probably itching for purpose—for a passion—for a quest. I've thought a lot about passion, about what it is that makes people so followable, successful, or electable. I wrote a lot of that down in a book called *Lose Your Cool.* (Feel free to borrow a copy from the library or rent it on your e-reader.) In it, I explained how everyone I know is interested in a couple of specific things:

1. Spirituality (not "religion" because it's hip to hate *that* now)
2. Helping people or contributing to good causes (also hip)

I know a lot of people who think Jesus was a pretty good guy. In the same way, a lot of my friends own TOMS shoes or wear To Write Love on Her Arms shirts in order to feel like they're a part of something. And that's not a bad thing.

But . . . how many people who say "Jesus was a good man; nothing more" would be willing to take a bullet in the head for his teachings? How many?

The answer, from almost everyone I've asked, is . . . zero. None.

Nobody who is merely interested in something would die for it. Which raises the question: What does it take for someone to die for something?

It takes passion.

What's the difference between interest and passion? *Action.*

It's the gateway. If you are only interested in something and then decide to get involved, you choose to sacrifice—to make a greater investment. You are then connected at a deeper level. Passion is what causes people to give up blood and sweat and tears for something.

In the Arthurian legend, Gareth had to step up and say, "I'll lay my life on the line for that purpose." He heard Lynette run down the list of dangerous foes. He knew what he was up against. But he went anyway. Because he wanted to be knighted. He believed in greater honor. He wanted to defend someone who was being held against her will. This isn't a story about how he was strong because he was a man, or how Lynette's sister couldn't help herself. It's a story about a kid who knew what he wanted to do and worked for it. He had a passion for justice and service and was willing to do anything to get there.

JUST START

You may have a big dream. A very big dream. Or you may have goals you're setting for this next semester or the next chapter in your career. But maybe you feel inadequate or underqualified.

Because I suffered with anxiety when I was in elementary school, I was an extremely unlikely person to be doing any of what I'm doing today. I wasn't the "right choice" to stand up in front of people and speak about slavery. Honestly, the first time I addressed the students at my school, I thought I was going to pass out. I felt like all the blood had drained from my head. I'm already really pale. I must've looked almost transparent that day.

A twelve-year-old kid with anxiety standing in front of the whole school telling stories about modern-day slaves? And asking everyone in the school to get involved by bringing in cups filled with loose change? How could that ever work? But it did. Dozens of kids caught the vision and volunteered to help out. In the end, after a two-week campaign, we had raised nearly ten thousand dollars, which we donated to an organization called International Justice Mission that sent rescuers to developing countries to free slaves. Seeing that success fueled my passion even more, but it never would have happened if I hadn't tried.

Part of persevering is just getting started. It is saying, "I'm ready to do this, despite whatever weaknesses I have or what people may have said to try to keep me down." You can't keep going if you haven't even started.

You might simply need to pick a time and place to announce your cause, your quest. You need to have identified some steps that make sense as a path to complete it. But when you're ready, you need to step up and say, "Here's what I'm going to do. Who wants to join me?"

Maybe your dream isn't this concrete; maybe it's not related to a specific cause, field of study, sport, or instrument. That's fine, because you don't have to know what you'll be doing every day for the rest of your life. We can all pursue the biggest, grandest, most overarching quest of all as we sort out our specific passions.

Here's the thing: I want to be passionate about loving God and loving my neighbor more than I love myself. The point of everything I've said in this book can pretty much be summed up in that. If our quest is only to obey all of the rules, we will feel exhausted and unfulfilled. These things have to change us from the inside out. That transformation is a continual process that will take time and some work. Studying good teaching plus avoiding content and activities that numb us. Looking for beauty everywhere and seeking God and opportunities to help others. Living humbly. All of that takes perseverance, too, because people will try to discourage you if you seem to have purpose, if you seem to have something a little bit figured out.

My advice: don't let them. Don't let people discourage you because you seem different or because they don't understand how you are wired or because they don't see your vision. Be humble, recognizing that your talents are a gift. But also be confident in whatever you have as a gifting, trusting that it's there for a reason.

It's my experience that people, especially those who mask insecurity with an over-the-top personality, will say and do awful things to try to make themselves feel better. In the story of Sir Gareth, you may have had a hard time believing that Lady Lynette could have been so mean, even after he proved himself at the beginning of the journey. Some people just won't understand your goals, your motivation, and your commitment to your quest, and they'll think they can break you. But hey, I believe in you. That may seem weird or empty since we've never met, but if you're human, and the type of human who would pick up and read this kind of book, I think there's something to you. You can do it.

WHEN YOU FEEL LIKE GIVING UP

I have friends who lift weights or run a lot. They plan their workouts knowing they will feel like quitting a few minutes before the end. They often put together a playlist of pump-up music that makes them feel like action heroes so they can break through the last wall of their workout or run the last few blocks.

If you feel like giving up but you want the end result badly enough, you have to find a way to keep going. It is important to seek encouragement. Gareth was on the verge of losing his battle physically. He may have started to doubt himself, to get discouraged—his "heart began to fail him." And that was when help came from an unlikely and unexpected source. Lynette offered some much-needed words of encouragement. About time, huh?

So whatever your quest, figure out what motivates you to keep going when you start to get down or tired. Is it rewards? "If I make it to the end of my run without stopping, I'll reward myself with a caramel macchiato at Starbucks." Or is it words of encouragement? Then find a friend or mentor who has the gift of encouragement, and don't be embarrassed to say, "I'm feeling discouraged today, so I was wondering if we could talk."

Some people really underestimate the power of motivation and encouragement to help them complete their quests. Don't fall into that trap. We all have days when we need an emotional pick-me-up, a bit of inspiration to help us persevere. There are countless stories of those who have found the strength to go on because of simple acts of encouragement: a letter from home during war, a pep talk before taking to the field in the final minutes of a game, a supportive word from a parent when school seemed too hard, a hug from a close friend that puts the pain or the challenge in perspective.

Maybe it's not so much about giving up as it is about giving up control.

Many businesses and ministries experience "founder's syndrome" after a few years (or decades) in operation. The person whose vision led to the creation of an organization that has been wildly successful now seems out of touch with the constituents and the challenges that threaten the mission. If the founder remains, the entire business or ministry is at risk. But if he or she is asked to leave, it could tear the whole operation apart.

So how do we know when to step away, to hand off the baton and let others manage something we've created? Only by seeking wisdom from God and those we trust to tell us the truth. If we evaluate their words and their message humbly and pray for guidance, we'll know when it's time to walk away.

I hope you don't see this as conflicting with the chapter's main message: not giving up in pursuit of a quest. Even if we do everything else this chapter discusses and make progress over the course of many years, we still may not accomplish our vision. But that's okay, as long as we've been faithful to take the steps toward the goal as God leads us.

I've heard stories about missionaries who have lived and served among the same tribespeople for years, never seeing one person decide to accept their teachings. Does that mean those missionaries weren't successful or faithful in the quest? Not in my opinion.

In the Torah, we see that even ancient Israel's great leader Moses had to forgo the accomplishment of his quest: entering the Promised Land. He had led his people out of slavery in Egypt and helped keep them alive for forty years in the middle of the desert. But Moses had also disobeyed God once along the way, so God told him he couldn't actually go into the new land. When the people finally reached the border of their new home, God said it was time to hand the reins to someone else: Joshua.

Does that mean Moses failed? Some would say yes; others, no. But by scriptural accounts Moses was a good leader who accomplished great things for God's people. In the end, he had no option but to "retire." It was his time. And the biblical record shows no evidence of him going kicking and screaming, whining and crying, being dragged by angels. He went voluntarily to a retirement party for two. God let him look into the new land—kind of a vision of the fulfillment of his quest. And then Moses was relieved of his duties. Joshua took over and did a great job leading Israel into its next chapter.

May it be the same for us when we have pursued with passion the God-inspired quest to which we have given our time, energy, and life. Some of us may actually get to see the quest fulfilled completely, like finding a cure for cancer, eradicating malaria, or eliminating slavery from the face of the earth. Others may be called to step away before the quest is completed. But for the time we are granted, let's be responsible, let us pursue our quest with wholehearted passion, tenacious perseverance, and transcendent love. Let us be guided always with the knowledge and the vision that love "always protects, always trusts, always hopes, always perseveres."[3]

ONWARD:
LIVING THE CODE

I n medieval times, those who became knights were a breed apart. They were honorable and highly regarded, even revered. They lived in a way that commanded respect. They held certain values as nonnegotiables—specific things they would always do, or never do. If they lived in modern times and dressed and looked like us, I believe they would still stand out. Why? Because the honorable traits and standards of chivalry that the knights lived by are just as rare today as they were back then. Perhaps even more so.

That's the kind of person I want to be—and it's consistent with the person I try to pattern my life after: Jesus. As you look back on the content of these chapters, I hope you're asking the same questions I did as I wrote it: "What's the right thing to do in this area?" "What does chivalrous living require?" And perhaps most important, "What needs to change inside of me?"

In this book I've written about issues that many educated philosophers, theologians, and therapists have dedicated their lives to studying. Please know that I don't consider myself any of those things. I know and understand that I'm a college guy, just starting on this journey of adulthood, and I have much to learn. In *Chivalry*, I've attempted to share some of the things I'm discovering along the way—and some of the things I hope to grow into. My views may change as I learn more. I hope my thoughts will help you, but I'd also encourage you to surround yourself with people wiser than you—mentors, teachers, parents, friends—to help you sort through the topics in the book.

This next section is designed to help you take the ideas I've shared and begin to implement them in your life. And if you'd like to do some serious considering of what it means to be chivalrous and even commit to a code of honor that would mark your life, I've provided some tools to make that happen.

In the following pages, you'll find some questions you can do on your own or with a small group. At the end of each section, you'll have an opportunity to commit to each principle of chivalry. I've even included a blank page at the end, where you can personalize this code by writing your own pledge.

For those of you who would like a more formal journey into a life of chivalry, please see www.zachhunter.me, where you can learn about Chivalry Camp and how to create some iconic and visual reminders of your commitment to this code.

PLEASE HEAR ME ON THIS. While this section provides practical commitments, the most important thing you can do is ask yourself the questions for each chapter. Be sensitive to what God may be leading you to consider in your life. I really don't want this to be an empty religious exercise for anyone or a white-knuckled commitment to try harder. It has become popular in the Christian community to take pledges and oaths with little discussion about the internal growth and maturity that leads us to fulfilling those commitments. In reality, it is God's work that transforms us to become more chivalrous. So the motivation for each commitment must be a desire to see God work within us. And we always have to leave room for grace—for God's continuing work in us as we blow it from time to time.

I. I WILL NOT GO ON THIS JOURNEY ALONE.

PERSONAL QUEST

1. Respond to these ideas: "I feel like I do better when I deal with challenges alone." "I have a hard time coping with difficult things alone." "I find myself running to my friends for support." Which statement best describes your personality?

2. The story of Carlos gives a picture of the value of having a diverse group of trusted friends. Have you cultivated this in your life? Where do you feel you need to be "staked"? Name some peers and some older mentors whom you can ask to join you on your journey.

3. When do you find yourself hiding from those who know you best? What makes you avoid conversations, not return messages, etc.?

4. As you get older and become independent, how can you ensure you're in relationships that move beyond accountability questions toward more transparent, honest discussions of mutual benefit?

5. Have you ever thought you could manage your life on your own? Do you get defensive when people offer you constructive criticism? You may be dealing with pride. Take a few minutes and ask God to uncover any prideful tendencies in you. Also ask him to direct you to people you can trust to walk with you.

LIVING THE CODE *Consider printing out the code below by downloading it on www.zachhunter.me under "Chivalry." Tape it to your mirror, keep it in your Bible, or put it some other place where you are likely to see it regularly.*

I. I WILL NOT GO ON THIS JOURNEY ALONE.

I do believe there is safety in traveling with friends. I believe I can find out more about myself by trusting comrades to share with me where I need to improve and to be there for me in tough times.

TODAY, I COMMIT MYSELF TO GROW TO BE MORE CHIVALROUS.

- I will purposefully invite trusted individuals to join me on my journey.

- I will submit myself to at least one mentor who is older and wiser than me and will ask that person to influence my life.

- I will seek the truth about myself from people I can trust— always weighing their words against what I know to be true.

- In times of fatigue, stress, or hurt, I will not run away from my friends and advisors. Instead I will seek them out, let them know I'm struggling, and ask for their support.

- Ultimately I will ask God to uncover in me any hidden pride or attitudes that make me isolate myself.

I commit myself to humbly seeking the help of the Holy Spirit to live out this chivalrous life.

_____   _____
Signature   Date

II. I WILL NEVER ATTACK FROM BEHIND.

PERSONAL QUEST

Take a few minutes to ponder these questions. Really let them sink in. As we mature in our faith and in our lives in general, some of the most important questions are the ones we ask ourselves.

1. Why do you sometimes criticize others? Are you gaining something from their pain? What does this say about how you see yourself?

2. When you are hanging out with people and they begin to talk about someone else in an unfavorable way, how do you react? Are you passive, or do you stop the conversation? Do you let it slide so you don't hurt your friends' feelings or so they don't think badly of you?

3. When you hear someone gossiping about a person who is not there, how can or should you react?

4. Think about the comments you've made today; how many of them were negative? Is it easier to think of a critique or a negative comment than it is to think of a compliment? What can you do to change this habit of negativity?

5. What do you say when someone makes you angry? What is your natural reaction?

6. When people hurt you, what can you do to control your natural tendency to fight back or to hurt their reputation or feelings? In that type of situation, you can only control how you react. What will you do?

7. How do you deal with the aftereffect of being hurt by gossip?

8. If you were to change the way you spoke about others, would that change the way you think? If so, how?

9. How often do you take the easy way out in tough conversations? Are you texting or messaging, instead of speaking face-to-face? If so, what's one step you can take to change that pattern?

Look back over the questions. Place an asterisk by the ones where you really felt God prompting you that something needed to change. Based upon your answers, write a declaration here about what you want to see changed in your life.

LIVING THE CODE *Consider printing out the code below by downloading it on www.zachhunter.me under "Chivalry." Tape it to your mirror, keep it in your Bible, or put it in some other place where you are likely to see it regularly.*

II. I WILL NEVER ATTACK FROM BEHIND.

It is my desire to avoid rumors, gossip, and sarcasm. To be kind to everyone, including those who are cruel to me. To pay back curses with blessings.

TODAY, I COMMIT MYSELF TO GROW TO BE MORE CHIVALROUS.

- I will not be a gossip merchant who criticizes or spreads rumors about people.

- I will not use humor or sarcasm to hurt others.

- I will be kind to everyone, even to those who insult or hurt me.

- I will pay back curses with blessings.

I commit myself to humbly seeking the help of the Holy Spirit to live out this chivalrous life.

_____

Signature   Date

III. I WILL PRACTICE SELF-CONTROL AND SELFLESSNESS.

PERSONAL QUEST

Before you forget about the things in this chapter that got under your skin—in a good way—take a few minutes to think them through. Hopefully these questions will help.

1. How do you respond to being told what *not* to do?

2. What do you think of the idea of purposefully delaying gratification—like waiting for dessert, or delaying playing video games or watching a movie until you finish an unpleasant task?

3. Do you find it hard to control your use of media? If so, have you talked with anyone about it? What are some steps you can take to get this under control?

4. How are you doing overall managing your self-control? Do you struggle with saying things you know you shouldn't say? Do you spend your time in ways that are unproductive? Are you putting things into your body that are not good for you?

5. What areas of your life do you need to begin making sacrifices in?

LIVING THE CODE *Consider printing out the code below by downloading it on www.zachhunter.me under "Chivalry." Tape it to your mirror, keep it in your Bible, or put it some other place where you are likely to see it regularly.*

III. I WILL PRACTICE SELF-CONTROL AND SELFLESSNESS.

In my journey toward chivalry, I want to see my self-control grow while my self-indulgence, selfishness, and self-consciousness shrink back and submit.

TODAY, I COMMIT MYSELF TO GROW TO BE MORE CHIVALROUS.

- I will control my desires, not be controlled by them.
- I will practice self-discipline so I can live without regrets.
- I will cultivate the fruit of self-control.
- I will transcend my selfish human nature and focus on serving others.
- I will surrender my pride and sacrifice my needs for the common good.

I understand it is impossible to fulfill this commitment apart from God's help. He is the one who transforms me so I can be more self-controlled. I commit myself to humbly seeking the help of the Holy Spirit to live out a life of chivalry.

_____

Signature   *Date*

IV. I WILL RESPECT LIFE AND FREEDOM.

PERSONAL QUEST

It's easy to read something and be moved. Or sometimes even to have our conscience moved in a way that prompts us to respond. But we're so conditioned to jump ahead quickly that we often forget what that quiet voice inside us was saying. That might be the voice of God's Spirit. Take a few minutes to be quiet and concentrate on these questions.

1. How are you investing your freedom? How could you better invest it?

2. "You can readily recall, can't you, how at one time the more you did just what you felt like doing—not caring about others, not caring about God—the worse your life became and the less freedom you had? And how much different is it now as you live in God's freedom, your lives healed and expansive in holiness?" (Romans 6:19, *The Message*). How has following God freed you?

3. Take an honest look at your life. How can you set good boundaries for yourself that might help give you freedom?

4. How does knowing what God thinks of life—that he delighted to make it—affect or change how you think about life?

LIVING THE CODE *Consider printing out the code below by downloading it on www.zachhunter.me under "Chivalry." Tape it to your mirror, keep it in your Bible, or put it some other place where you are likely to see it regularly.*

IV. I WILL RESPECT LIFE AND FREEDOM.

I recognize that my freedom—especially my spiritual freedom—came at a price. I believe all life is a gift and should be honored.

TODAY, I COMMIT MYSELF TO GROW TO BE MORE CHIVALROUS.

- I will defend the dignity of every person.
- I will respect those whom others may view as less valuable—the poor, the elderly, the unborn, the sick or disabled.
- I will remind myself of my freedom and fight for the freedom of others.
- I will invest my freedom, and I will not take advantage of my spiritual freedom (the freedom I have because of Christ) to cause others to stumble.
- I will be civil with those with whom I disagree.

I am grateful for my ability to live a life of freedom. I commit myself to humbly seeking the help of the Holy Spirit to live a life of chivalry.

_____

Signature   Date

V. I WILL FIGHT ONLY FOR THE SAKE OF THOSE WHO ARE UNABLE TO DEFEND THEMSELVES, OR IN THE DEFENSE OF JUSTICE.

PERSONAL QUEST

Justice has become a buzzword in our generation. But has our focus on justice "out there" allowed us to feel we are free from being just in our personal relationships and in our own neighborhoods? Take a few minutes to consider these questions, and ask God to give you greater sensitivity to blind spots you may have in your life.

1. Do you find yourself swinging a sword in defense of things that don't matter? Petty arguments? Your own reputation? Or do you fight for God's reputation and for the sake of others?

2. What was the topic of your last argument or disagreement? Did it have eternal consequences?

3. Do you think violence is ever okay? The next time you are faced with injustice, how do you hope you will handle it?

4. What are you leading with? What are your actions and words communicating to others? What are your thoughts on the statement: "The first thing out of Jesus' mouth was often a question—not a judgment call" (see page 75)?

5. What principles do you think are worth fighting for?

6. How do you treat the people closest to you? How can you demonstrate love this week to someone close to you—and also to someone you don't know or who is different from you?

LIVING THE CODE *Consider printing out the code below by downloading it on www.zachhunter.me under "Chivalry." Tape it to your mirror, keep it in your Bible, or put it in some other place where you are likely to see it regularly.*

V. I WILL FIGHT ONLY FOR THE SAKE OF THOSE WHO ARE UNABLE TO DEFEND THEMSELVES, OR IN THE DEFENSE OF JUSTICE.

I recognize that it is easiest to defend myself and my own rights and that it's often difficult to speak up for someone else when it might cost me something. My desire is to lead with love and to be a person who brings justice and protection to others.

TODAY, I COMMIT MYSELF TO GROW TO BE MORE CHIVALROUS.

- I will lead first with love rather than judgment.
- I will rid myself of hatred and keep my heart in check, so hatred and bitterness cannot grow.
- I will stand up for those who are unable to defend themselves, including those who are bullied, treated as outcasts, or viewed as inferior in some way.
- I will view violence as the last resort.
- I will ask God to reveal racism and bigotry that may be buried in my heart.
- I will be a peacemaker.

I want justice to be a hallmark of my life. I want to be seen as a gracious defender of others. I commit myself to humbly seeking the help of the Holy Spirit to live a life of chivalry.

_____

Signature   *Date*

VI. I WILL HONOR TRUTH AND ALWAYS KEEP MY PROMISES.

PERSONAL QUEST

Consider these questions to gain insight into areas where you might be struggling to live chivalrously, to be truthful, or to keep your word.

1. How do you think Carl should have acted or responded differently in the prom story?

2. Do you ever lie or exaggerate when you first meet people in an effort to relate to them or make them like you?

3. What is the difference between being truthful and being blunt?

4. How do you present your own opinion as fact and call it the truth?

5. Being blunt or straightforward can be good. But sharing the truth insensitively will hinder people from learning from it because they will be focused on the hurt instead of the truth. How can you be intentional about sharing the truth in love?

6. How often do you shy away from being completely honest with your friends because you are afraid to hurt them? Is that being a true friend? What are the exceptions?

7. Why do we tell people that we will do something or pray for them and then *not do it*?

8. Why do you think people lie or exaggerate?

9. Are you known for keeping your word, or would friends say you often bail out on commitments?

LIVING THE CODE *Consider printing out the code below by downloading it on www.zachhunter.me under "Chivalry." Tape it to your mirror, keep it in your Bible, or put it some other place where you are likely to see it regularly.*

VI. I WILL HONOR TRUTH AND ALWAYS KEEP MY PROMISES.

I do not want to become casual about keeping my word and telling the truth. It's easy to lie in a quick text or to neglect to answer a message. I want to seek truth in all circumstances and work hard to honor my commitments.

TODAY, I COMMIT MYSELF TO GROW TO BE MORE CHIVALROUS.

- I will be truthful.

- I will not use the truth as a weapon by being brutally honest or pointing out faults that don't need to be highlighted.

- I will keep my commitments, even when it's not convenient.

- As much as it's in my power, I will not make promises unless I know I can keep them.

- I will not exaggerate my own strengths, experience, or contacts.

I want to be known as trustworthy—the kind of person others can count on. I want to avoid telling lies or exaggerating. I commit myself to humbly seeking the help of the Holy Spirit to live out a life of chivalry.

_____

Signature   *Date*

VII. I WILL FEAR NO EVIL.

PERSONAL QUEST

Some people appear to be fearless. But most of us, if we're honest, have secret fears. Maybe these questions will help you uncover your perspective on what you fear—and what evil really is.

1. What's your biggest fear?

2. What is the worst that could happen if your greatest fear came true? Where would God be in the midst of that worst-case scenario?

3. What keeps you stuck in the "cave" of fear?

4. Are you afraid of people who are different from you? Do you ever view those people as evil, just because they are from a different part of the world or have a different skin color or religion? If so, why?

5. If you made an effort to be friendly to "them," what do you think would happen?

6. Do you think it is okay to wonder and ask hard questions? Why or why not?

7. How do you perceive God? Is he easily angered or too sensitive? Is he all-knowing and all-powerful? Is he big enough to handle all your questions?

8. If you could ask one bold question of God, what would it be?

LIVING THE CODE *Consider printing out the code below by downloading it on www.zachhunter.me under "Chivalry." Tape it to your mirror, keep it in your Bible, or put it some other place where you are likely to see it regularly.*

VII. I WILL FEAR NO EVIL.

The world is a scary place. In fact, the evil in the world makes it pretty clear that this is not really my home. I am an alien here. But if I trust God while I'm here, I can live at peace and without fear of evil.

TODAY, I COMMIT MYSELF TO GROW TO BE MORE CHIVALROUS.

- I will not call things evil simply because they are unfamiliar or uncomfortable to me.

- I will submit my fears to God's perfect love, knowing it is the ultimate way to overcome fear.

- I will not run away from situations that cause me anxiety just to protect myself.

- I will ask God to give me courage and to help me rise above my fears.

- I will acknowledge genuine evil and live in a way that reflects Jesus.

I want to be free of fear, and I want to be a person who doesn't vilify people who are different from me. My desire is to live courageously and to walk a life free to love others and free of the bondage of fear. I commit myself to humbly seeking the help of the Holy Spirit to live a life of chivalry.

_____

Signature   *Date*

VIII. I WILL ALWAYS FOLLOW THE LAW UNLESS IT GOES AGAINST WHAT IS MORAL AND GOOD.

PERSONAL QUEST

1. What does it look like to live lawfully? What changes do you need to make to live rightly under the law?

2. In what areas of your life do you feel you are above the law? When or where do you justify doing wrong?

3. Discuss or write your thoughts on C. S. Lewis's perspective on universal morality: "There is nothing indulgent about the Moral Law. It is as hard as nails. It tells you to do the straight thing and it does not seem to care how painful, or dangerous, or difficult it is to do." Do you think that we have an innate sense of right and wrong? What does that imply concerning a Creator and man as a created being?

4. If you had been in Audrey Hepburn's situation, what do you think you would have done? Why? Are there still situations today when you think you should act as she did?

5. "The creeds and promises and rules bring joy and fulfillment only when they overflow from a heart that has been changed by the scandalous love of Jesus" (page 140). What is the condition of your heart?

6. Think of a time, past or present, when you have disagreed with someone in authority. Did you handle it well? Or do you wish you had acted differently? Was it a positive experience? What could have made it more honoring and productive?

7. Respond to this quote by Audrey Hepburn: "It's that wonderful old-fashioned idea that others come first and you come second. This was the whole ethic by which I was brought up. Others matter more than you do, so 'don't fuss, dear; get on with it.'"[1] How is this similar or different from your perspective?

LIVING THE CODE *Consider printing the code below by downloading it on www.zachhunter.me under "Chivalry." Tape it to your mirror, keep it in your Bible, or put it some other place where you are likely to see it regularly.*

VIII. I WILL ALWAYS FOLLOW THE LAW UNLESS IT GOES AGAINST WHAT IS MORAL AND GOOD.

I am sometimes tempted to make moral compromises and overlook the law of the land because I view parts of it as insignificant. Speeding, pirating music or movies, or taking something that doesn't belong to me are common examples. But there may be times when my devotion to Jesus might require that I disobey the law or rules instituted by my school or community in order to do what is right. In these situations, I can pray and trust God for wisdom.

TODAY, I COMMIT MYSELF TO GROW TO BE MORE CHIVALROUS.

- I will obey the law unless it goes against what is moral and good.

- I will not excuse or justify my behavior if I am breaking the law of the land or God's law.

- I will not give in to peer pressure to break the law, whether by using illegal substances, pirating music, or joining other behaviors often viewed as culturally acceptable.

- I will be respectful of authorities placed over me.

- I will ask God to prepare me to disobey the law or rules that may be immoral or go against his commands.

I want to be a person of integrity. I commit myself to humbly seeking the help of the Holy Spirit to live a life of chivalry.

_____   _____
Signature   Date

IX. I WILL LIVE AND DIE WITH HONOR.

PERSONAL QUEST

It can be easy to just go through the motions day after day. But God created us to live abundantly, and he has extravagantly given us his love. One mark of Christians should be that we live lives of honor and gratefulness—and enthusiasm, believing that life is a gift.

1. Evaluate your life and attitudes. Are you truly living or just ticking off the days? If you are struggling or have lost your joy, find someone trustworthy (maybe a mentor, pastor, or counselor) with whom you can talk.

2. Have you been hurt in the past? Are you clinging to bitterness? If so, how is this impacting you?

3. Do you think your past hurts entitle you to special treatment by others? How does this show up in your life?

4. Are there areas of your life where your thoughts or behavior are destructive? These may not be big things, but they may include areas that have long-term impact. Who can you talk to about them?

LIVING THE CODE *Consider printing the code below by downloading it on www.zachhunter.me under "Chivalry." Tape it to your
mirror, keep it in your Bible, or put it some other place where you
are likely to see it regularly.*

IX. I WILL LIVE AND DIE WITH HONOR.

*Life is a precious gift—one to be respected and valued. I don't want
to waste my days.*

TODAY, I COMMIT MYSELF TO GROW TO BE MORE CHIVALROUS.

- I will not take my life for granted but will remind myself
  of the things I have to be grateful for.

- I will ask my mentors and friends to help me fight the
  cynicism that erodes my joy and gratefulness.

- I will seek professional help if I find myself losing my joy
  over an extended period of time, or if I ever find myself
  thinking or doing something destructive.

*There is an enemy of my soul who wants to steal my joy and who
envies the abundant life God gives his followers. I will submit myself
to humbly seek the Holy Spirit's help in resisting the enemy and
living a life of chivalry.*

_____

Signature   Date

X. I WILL NEVER ABANDON MY QUEST.

PERSONAL QUEST

Before you wrap up the final chapter in Chivalry, *think through what it's going to take to sustain your commitments. Maybe these questions will help.*

1. What did you think about the story of Prince Gareth and Lady Lynette? What would you have done if you were in Gareth's shoes? Would you have continued on the quest?

2. Gareth was able to remain focused on his quest even though everyone around him—including the person he was helping— was fighting against him. How can you persevere in your quest? What are some ways you can look past present adversity and remain focused on your cause?

3. When you feel like giving up, what are some things you can do to keep going? Name several people you can always look to for encouragement.

4. Do you discredit the little jobs? How have you seen opportunity open because you were willing to start with such jobs?

5. Are you afraid to begin your quest? How can you keep from getting discouraged by the size of your quest when you're still at the starting gate?

6. When you hand over control to someone else, do you view that as giving up? How can the best way to continue the quest sometimes be to hand it off to the next person?

LIVING THE CODE *Consider printing the code below by down-loading it on www.zachhunter.me under "Chivalry." Tape it to your mirror, keep it in your Bible, or put it some other place where you are likely to see it regularly.*

X. I WILL NEVER ABANDON MY QUEST.

There will be days when I feel like giving up. My commitment may wane, and I might get weary of being the person who wants to do the right thing. But a life of chivalry is a lifelong commitment. I want to submit to Jesus and allow him to transform my life.

TODAY, I COMMIT MYSELF TO GROW TO BE MORE CHIVALROUS.

- I want to be known as someone who doesn't avoid difficult or thankless jobs and will purposefully seek positions that allow me to grow.

- I will serve others—including those from whom I have nothing to gain.

- I will seek counsel when I feel like giving up.

- I will persevere even when I face challenges or when I'm tired and feel like giving up.

- I will ask others to help me accurately evaluate my work ethic, my commitment to perseverance, and my dedication to finding my own passion and calling.

When things get difficult in life, I will remember the patience God has toward me. I'll also remember that Jesus was a man familiar with suffering who always persevered, even when in relationships with difficult people and when facing insurmountable challenges. I commit myself to humbly seeking the help of the Holy Spirit to live a life of chivalry.

Signature   Date

WRITE YOUR OWN PLEDGE HERE:

What's on your mind? What stuck in your heart? Maybe reading this book triggered something in you that I didn't even talk about. What else do you want to remember as you continue your quest?

_____

TODAY, I COMMIT MYSELF TO GROW TO BE MORE CHIVALROUS.

-

-

-

-

_____

Signature   *Date*

PROVISIONS
FOR THE JOURNEY

MIXTAPE

Music is an important part of my life—it inspires me and causes me to think. Here are a few albums for our journey, including some of the music I listened to while writing this book. You can also check www.zachhunter.me for updates to the mixtape. I'd love to hear your music suggestions as well. You can submit them on my Facebook page (www.facebook.com/zachhunterofficial) or Twitter page (www.twitter.com/zachjhunter).

> *Triangle* by Slow Magic
> *Bleu Bird Instrumentals* by Customary
> *Valtari* by Sigur Rós
> *Pocketless Souls* by Je'Kob
> *The Sounds of Daniel Bashta* by Daniel Bashta

ART

Throughout the book, you'll find art and quotes you can use in social media or print out and use in your room or locker. To find more, go to www.zachhunter.me and click on "Chivalry." There you'll find a lot of downloads free for your use!

COMPANIONS

I'm an avid reader and find companions through the books and authors who have meant something in my life. Some are biographies of people who have already died; some are fictional pieces or works of poetry. Below are a couple of my recommendations that informed some of my thinking as I was writing this book. For more, visit my website at www.zachhunter.me.

Books

Pilgrim at Tinker Creek by Annie Dillard
Narrative of the Life of Frederick Douglass by Frederick
   Douglass
The Sacred Echo by Margaret Feinberg

Films

Amazing Grace (2006)
Heima (2007)
Henry Poole Is Here (2008)
To Save a Life (2009)

Artists

Scott Erickson (www.scottericksonart.com)
David Bean (www.visualreserve.com)
Jonathan Huang (http://jonathan-huang.com/)

SHOUT OUTS

I'd love to give a big shout out to all of the following people who helped in the process of writing this book.

Mom and Dad for helping with research, editing, and writing questions. I appreciate and love you guys.

Thanks, Nate, for being the coolest little brother ever.

Shout outs to cafe 304—love you guys. (And all of KC 3.)

Slow Magic—I love you like a brother. Jonas—you are my favorite samurai.

Thank you, Hannah and Emily, for helping out with questions. You girls rock.

Love you, sweet MLE. It's an honor to be able to spend the rest of my life with you.

Thanks to Cozette, Jordan N., Jordan L. R., Steve Carter, and Randy Rainwater for helping flesh out some of the ideas in this project. CDT, Nishan David, Leighton—you are three of the best brothers from other mothers that I could ask for.

To the team at Tyndale Momentum—thank you for believing in this project and giving me a place to express what I've been learning. Jan, Yolanda, Sarah, Nancy, Erin, and my editor, Jeremy, I appreciate you sticking with this until we got it right. Dean, thank you for creating a cover and layout I really like.

And, to the person reading this—there are so many things you could be doing with your time. It is humbling to know you would choose to read this book. Thank you for supporting this project.

ENDNOTES

AN EPIC QUEST

1. Tavis Smiley and Cornel West, *The Rich and the Rest of Us: A Poverty Manifesto* (New York: Smiley Books, 2012), 135.

II: I WILL NEVER ATTACK FROM BEHIND.

1. See John 4:17-18.
2. Leviticus 19:18
3. Analects of Confucius, 15:24, quoted in *Encyclopedia of Religion and Society*, William H. Swatos Jr., ed. (Walnut Creek, CA: AltaMira Press, 1998), 116.
4. Matthew 7:12
5. See Matthew 15:1-14.
6. Matthew 15:15-20
7. See Matthew 12:34, NIV.
8. See Matthew 5:39.

III: I WILL PRACTICE SELF-CONTROL AND SELFLESSNESS.

1. Anthony St. Peter, *The Greatest Quotations of All Time* (2010: Xlibris, n.p.), 164, http://www.finestquotes.com/author_quotes-author-William%20 Arthur%20Ward-page-0.htm#ixzz2C2ARtoqU.
2. Matthew 7:16-18, NIV
3. Bill Watterson, *Calvin and Hobbes*, July 10, 1987, http://www.gocomics.com /calvinandhobbes/1987/07/10.
4. 1 Kings 3:16-28

IV: I WILL RESPECT LIFE AND FREEDOM.

1. Frederick Douglass, *Narrative of the Life of Frederick Douglass* (New York: Dover Publications, 1995), 43. Unabridged republication of *Narrative of the Life of Frederick Douglass, an American Slave*, originally published in 1845.
2. Ibid., 71–72.
3. Amos 5:21-24, THE MESSAGE (italics in the original)

4. Romans 5:20-21, THE MESSAGE (italics in the original)
5. Romans 6:1-3, THE MESSAGE
6. Romans 6:15-18, THE MESSAGE (italics in the original)
7. See 1 Corinthians 6:12.
8. You can listen to Judah Smith's sermon "Mistaken Love" online at www.myspace.com/judahsmith/music/songs/mistaken-love-25408666.
9. See Genesis 2:18.
10. See Psalm 8:5 and Hebrews 2:7.
11. Shane Claiborne, *The Irresistible Revolution: Living As an Ordinary Radical,* (Grand Rapids: Zondervan, 2006), 44.
12. Check out Kid President at www.kidpresident.com.

V: I WILL FIGHT ONLY FOR THE SAKE OF THOSE WHO ARE UNABLE TO DEFEND THEMSELVES, OR IN THE DEFENSE OF JUSTICE.

1. "We are Christ's ambassadors; God is making his appeal through us. We speak for Christ when we plead, 'Come back to God!'" (2 Corinthians 5:20).
2. *The American Heritage Dictionary of the English Language,* 4th edition, s.v. "violence," accessed November 15, 2012, http://www.thefreedictionary.com /violence.
3. Mark Driscoll, quoted by Brandon O'Brien, "A Jesus for Real Men," *Christianity Today,* April 18, 2008, http://www.christianitytoday.com/ct/2008 /april/27.48.html.
4. Comment posted by Cheryl Hopper on July 27, 2012, in response to *God's Politics:* "The Myth of Redemptive Violence" blog entry by Shane Claiborne, July 24, 2012, http://sojo.net/blogs/2012/07/24/myth-redemptive-violence.
5. See Matthew 5:27-28.
6. See Matthew 5:21-22.
7. Ephesians 6:11-12, NIV
8. Hebrews 11:1, NIV
9. Hebrews 4:12, ASV
10. See Proverbs 16:18 and Matthew 26:52.
11. Attributed to Sir Edmund Burke.
12. Isaiah 1:17
13. Dara Fisk-Ekanger, "The Day Racism Hit Home," *Boundless* Webzine, December 13, 2000.
14. Ibid.

VI. I WILL HONOR TRUTH AND ALWAYS KEEP MY PROMISES.

1. Matthew Henry, *Matthew Henry's Commentary on the Whole Bible in One Volume,* Ed. Leslie F. Church (Grand Rapids: Regency Reference Library, 1960), 1818–1819, http://mhc.biblecommenter.com/1_corinthians/12.htm.
2. See Romans 10:9.

VII. I WILL FEAR NO EVIL.

1. 1 John 4:18, NIV
2. 1 John 4:16, NIV
3. *Merriam-Webster's Collegiate Dictionary*, 11th ed., s.v. "xenophobia."
4. *Wikipedia*, s.v. "anxiety disorder," last modified February 17, 2013, http://en.wikipedia.org/wiki/Anxiety_disorder.
5. See Romans 12:21.
6. C. S. Lewis, *The Screwtape Letters* (New York: HarperCollins, 1996), 59–61.
7. Timothy Snyder, "Hitler vs. Stalin: Who Killed More?" *The New York Review of Books*, March 10, 2011, http://www.nybooks.com/articles/archives/2011/mar/10/hitler-vs-stalin-who-killed-more/?pagination=false/.
8. C. S. Lewis, *Mere Christianity* (New York: HarperCollins, 1980), 44.
9. See Romans 12:21.

VIII. I WILL ALWAYS FOLLOW THE LAW UNLESS IT GOES AGAINST WHAT IS MORAL AND GOOD.

1. Lesley Garner, "Lesley Garner Meets the Legendary Actress as She Prepares for This Week's UNICEF Gala Performance," *The Sunday Telegraph*, May 26, 1991, posted on the website *Audrey Hepburn: A Tribute to Her Humanitarian Work*, http://www.ahepburn.com/article6.html.
2. Donald Spoto, *Enchantment: The Life of Audrey Hepburn* (New York: Crown Publishing Group, 2006), 27.
3. Ibid., 39.
4. Ibid., 26.
5. Barry Paris, *Audrey Hepburn* (New York: Berkeley Books, 1996), 21.
6. Ibid., 30.
7. Ibid., 32.
8. See http://www.history.com/topics/rwandan-genocide.
9. See Exodus 20:3-17.
10. Matthew 5:17, NIV.
11. Lewis, *Mere Christianity*, 30.
12. Ibid., 3–4, 26. Book I: The Law of Human Nature, "They say things like this: 'How'd you like it if anyone did the same to you?'—'That's my seat, I was there first'—'Leave him alone, he isn't doing you any harm'—'Why should you shove in first?'—'Give me a bit of your orange, I gave you a bit of mine'—'Come on, you promised.' People say things like that every day, educated people as well as uneducated, and children as well as grown-ups. Now what interests me about all these remarks is that the man who makes them is not merely saying that the other man's behaviour does not happen to please him. He is appealing to some kind of standard of behaviour which he expects the other man to know about. . . . It looks, in fact, very much as if both parties had in mind some kind of Law or Rule of fair play or decent behaviour or morality or whatever you like to call it, about which they really

agreed. And they have. . . . I am not yet within a hundred miles of the God of Christian theology. All I have got to is a Something which is directing the universe, and which appears in me as a law urging me to do right and making me feel responsible and uncomfortable when I do wrong."

13. William C. Placher, *Readings in the History of Christian Theology, Volume 2: From the Reformation to the Present* (Philadelphia: Westminster Press, 1988), 187, www.africa.upenn.edu/Articles_Gen/Letter_Birmingham.html.

14. See Matthew 22:35-40.

IX. I WILL LIVE AND DIE WITH HONOR.

1. C. S. Lewis, *The Problem of Pain* (New York: HarperCollins, 2001), 93–94. Originally published in 1940.

2. Ibid., 91.

3. Annie Dillard, *Pilgrim at Tinker Creek* (New York: Harper Perennial Modern Classics, 2007), 9.

4. Centers for Disease Control and Prevention, "10 Leading Causes of Death by Age Group, United States—2010," http://www.cdc.gov/injury/wisqars /pdf/10LCID_All_Deaths_By_Age_Group_2010-a.pdf.

X. I WILL NEVER ABANDON MY QUEST.

1. Alfred, Lord Tennyson, *Idylls of the King* (New York: Signet Classic, 2003), 60.

2. UrbanDictionary.com, s.v. "peon," http://www.urbandictionary.com /define.php?term=peon.

3. 1 Corinthians 13:7, NIV

LIVING THE CODE: DISCUSSION GUIDE AND PLEDGES

1. Spoto, *Enchantment*, 32.

ABOUT THE AUTHOR

ZACH HUNTER is a college student who is helping lead a new generation of activists to put their faith into action to address some of the most serious problems facing the world today.

In his debut book, *Be the Change* (2007), Zach profiles people who are investing in the world to make a difference. Zach's second book, *Generation Change* (2008), gives practical steps for students to take action and find solutions to real-world problems. In *Lose Your Cool* (2009), Zach challenges his peers to shed conventional ideas of what is cool and instead stoke a passion for what really matters. Zach has also written for *Boundless*, an online magazine for college students and twenty-somethings, and *Catalyst Groupzine*. He has partnered with artists in the Christian community to help raise awareness about human rights violations and the plight of the poor. Recently Zach spoke in Australia, Switzerland, Norway, Germany, and Canada, inspiring youth to make a difference. He also appeared at White House events and was honored by CNN as a modern-day hero.

While in seventh grade, Zach launched the Loose Change to Loosen Chains campaign, through which his school and youth group raised awareness and funds to help end modern-day slavery—a problem facing 27 million people worldwide. Today students around the globe are participating in the LC2LC campaign to benefit organizations involved in the abolition of slavery.

Currently a university student in Colorado, Zach spends his free time speaking to hundreds of thousands of people about God's heart for the hurting and oppressed, sharing his dream that his generation would discover God's great love for them and be motivated to care for their neighbors around the world. Zach also appears regularly on TV and radio and contributes to magazine and newspaper articles.

Zach contributed to the Just Start DVD curriculum, also featuring Chuck Colson, Desmond Tutu, Kay Warren, Joni Eareckson Tada, and others. Zach served as the global student spokesperson for The Amazing Change, a social justice campaign launched by Bristol Bay Productions in conjunction with the 2007 major motion picture *Amazing Grace*, based on the life of antislavery pioneer William Wilberforce. Zach has been featured in Pulitzer Prize–winning author Nicholas Kristof's book *Half the Sky*, in *Do Hard Things* by Alex and Brett Harris, and in the January 2008 edition of *Biography Today*, a magazine series about people that students should know in the world today. A children's book has been written about Zach as part of the Young Heroes series published by Cengage Learning. Zach also contributed to *You Were Made to Make a Difference* by Max Lucado and was featured in *Wrecked* by Jeff Goins and *Dating Delilah* by Judah Smith.

CONTINUE THE
CHIVALRY EXPERIENCE...

Visit www.zachhunter.me or scan the code below with your smartphone to access more *Chivalry* materials online, including videos with Zach.

www.tyndal.es/ZachHunter

WHAT OTHERS ARE SAYING ABOUT ZACH HUNTER AND HIS WORK

"A new generation of prophetic voices is emerging that understands (like the prophets of old) that God desires justice to roll like waters. Zach Hunter, at the age of fifteen, is one of those voices. We all need to listen."

JOHN ORTBERG
Menlo Park Presbyterian Church

"I am sure that when I was a teen I was navigating my world quite differently than Zach Hunter. Zach's life and words cry freedom with the force of William Wilberforce."

DAN HASELTINE
Jars of Clay and Blood Water Mission

"He is no longer a kid, but a young man; still passionate about seeing a generation use its gifts, talents, and passions to stand for peace, love, and justice."

JOEL HOUSTON
Hillsong United
(from the foreword for Zach's book *Lose Your Cool*)

221

"I love Zach's heart."
RANDY ALCORN
Bestselling author and speaker

"Zach Hunter is a brilliant social entrepreneur."
NICHOLAS D. KRISTOF
New York Times bestselling coauthor of *Half the Sky*;
Pulitzer Prize–winning columnist for the *New York Times*

"I'm excited and anxious to see what God is going to do through Zach. I can only imagine what change our generation can bring when we channel our attention and passion toward affecting this world for the Kingdom of God."
LEELAND MOORING
Recording artist

"I love Zach and his heart. At a young age he understands that once you've tasted purpose, it's really hard to be satisfied with mere existence. He's a leader in a growing group of young people who understands that our time on earth is a gift— they don't want to waste it."
JEFF FOXWORTHY
Comedian, author, and host of *Are You Smarter Than a Fifth Grader?*

To book Zach Hunter for a speaking engagement, please contact:
Loosechangetoloosenchains@gmail.com

YOUTH GROUPS → SCHOOLS → CHURCHES

LET US BRING OUR LIVE EVENT TO YOU!

Book a one-night-only Chivalry Camp or a two-day program. We can serve you with a turnkey event featuring Zach Hunter and our worship leaders, or Zach can speak to your group and work with your existing team.

And ask about the special Chivalry student-and-parent event that includes a dedication experience as we make a commitment to live out a code of honor.

For more information about booking, e-mail
CHIVALRYCAMP@GMAIL.COM.

Online Discussion *guide*

TAKE *your* TYNDALE READING EXPERIENCE *to the* NEXT LEVEL

A FREE discussion guide for this book is available at bookclubhub.net, perfect for sparking conversations in your book group or for digging deeper into the text on your own.

www.bookclubhub.net

You'll also find free discussion guides for other Tyndale books, e-newsletters, e-mail devotionals, virtual book tours, and more!